The Primary Teacher's Guide to

Spelling and Vocabulary

• Key subject knowledge • Background information • Teaching tips •

Book End, Range Road, Witney, Oxfordshire, OX29 0YD
www.scholastic.co.uk
© 2013 Scholastic Ltd
1 2 3 4 5 6 7 8 9   3 4 5 6 7 8 9 0 1 2

British Library Cataloguing-in-Publication Data
A catalogue record for this book is available from the
British Library.

ISBN 978-1407-12809-2
Printed and bound by CPI Group (UK) Ltd, Croydon,
CR0 4YY

Author
Paul Hollin

Editorial team
Rachel Morgan, Melissa Rugless,
Louise Titley, Gemma Carey

Indexer
Sue Lightfoot

Icons
Tomek.gr

Series Designers
Shelley Best and Sarah Garbett

Typesetter
Ricky Capanni (International Book Management)

Acknowledgements
The publishers gratefully acknowledge permission
to reproduce the following copyright material:

Oxford University Press for the use of the
definitions of 'spell', 'hotchpot', 'hotchpotch' and
'dictionary' from the *Concise Oxford Dictionary
10th Edition* edited by Judy Pearsall. Text © 2001,
Oxford University Press (2001, Oxford University
Press), and for the use of the thesaurus entry for
'thesaurus' from the *Oxford Thesaurus of English
3rd Edition*. Text © 2009, Oxford University Press
(2009, Oxford University Press).

Every effort has been made to trace copyright
holders for the works reproduced in this book,
and the publishers apologise for any inadvertent
omissions.

Contents

Icon key

Information within this book is highlighted in the margins by a series of different icons. They are:

Subject facts
Key subject knowledge is clearly presented and explained in this section.

Why you need to know these facts
Provides justification for understanding the facts that have been explained in the previous section.

Vocabulary
A list of key words, terms and language relevant to the preceding section. Vocabulary entries appear in the glossary.

Amazing facts
Interesting snippets of background knowledge to share.

Common misconceptions
Identifies and corrects some of the common misconceptions and beliefs that may be held about the subject area.

Teaching ideas
Outlines practical teaching suggestions using the knowledgeexplained in the preceding section.

Questions
Identifies common questions and provides advice on how to answer them.

Handy tips
Specific tips or guidance on best practice in the classroom.

Spelling and vocabulary

I take it you already know
Of tough and bough and cough and dough?
Others may stumble, but not you,
On hiccough, thorough, slough and through?
Well done! And now you wish, perhaps,
To learn of less familiar traps?
Beware of heard, a dreadful word
That looks like beard and sounds like bird,
And dead: it's said like bed, not bead –
For goodness sake don't call it deed!
Watch out for meat and great and threat
(They rhyme with suite and straight and debt).
A moth is not a moth in mother,
Nor both in bother, broth in brother,
And here is not a match for there
Nor dear and fear for bear and pear,
And then there's dose and rose and lose –
Just look them up – and goose and choose,
And cork and work and card and ward,
And font and front and word and sword,
And do and go and thwart and cart –
Come, come, I've hardly made a start!
A dreadful language? Man alive!
I'd mastered it when I was five.

Anon

No one is sure who wrote this whimsical poem highlighting the inconsistencies and absurdities of English spellings. Why do we have such a 'hotchpotch' language? There are clues everywhere: let's quickly examine *hotchpotch*. The *Oxford English Dictionary* (*OED*) tells us:

Hotchpotch *(N. Amer. Hodgepodge) > noun (in sing.)*
a confused mixture: a hotchpotch of uncoordinated services.
A mutton stew with mixed vegetables.
- ORIGIN late Middle English: variant of **HOTCHPOT**

Following the trail, we find *hotchpot* just before *hotchpotch*
in the *OED*:

Hotchpot *> noun* 1 *[mass noun] Law the reunion and blending*
together of properties for the purpose of securing equal division,
especially of the property of an intestate parent.
2 *variant spelling of* **HOTCHPOTCH**
- ORIGIN late Middle English (in sense 2): from Anglo-Norman
French and Old French hochepot, from hocher 'to shake' (probably
of Low German origin) + pot 'pot'.

What have we learned from this brief research?
- Hotchpotch is a noun.
- It is spelled differently in North America.
- It has more than one meaning.
- It is a variant on a different word (*hotchpot*), which also has another meaning.
- Its origin is late Middle English, from Anglo-Norman French and Old French, which in its turn borrowed from Low German.
- More importantly, we have also learned that English has a long and complex history, is changing as its usage moves around the world, and that dictionaries are powerful, knowledge-rich sources.

All of this information from a rarely used word: *hotchpotch*.
At least it is phonetic, meaning that anyone with a secure
grounding in phonic knowledge could write it. Alas, we cannot
say the same for all of the English language, where having a good
vocabulary does not guarantee a person good spelling skills. The
light-hearted verse on page 5 also has an alternative ending:

A dreadful language? Why, man alive,
I'd learned to talk it when I was five.
And yet to write it, the more I tried,
I hadn't learned it at fifty-five!

Maybe it is a bit excessive to suggest that children have mastered the speaking of English by the time they are five, but the main point is a reasonable one – English is a lot easier to speak than it is to read and write. The main reason for this is the complex and irregular nature of the English language, and even after decades of linguistic classification, schooling, research and government initiatives – not to mention the sweat and effort of countless thousands of teachers and children – the teaching and acceptable use of English still remains an area of public contention and pedagogic toil.

Why read this book?

Not only is English a complex language to teach, but the typical primary classroom will have maybe 30 (or more) children all with widely different vocabulary levels, language capabilities and cognitive abilities. There may also be children for whom English is a second language, and others with complex special needs.

Presuming that we all agree that a strong vocabulary and good levels of literacy are vitally important, this book aims to help teachers to deepen their background knowledge and to develop an effective range of classroom practices, by considering how children acquire language; explaining why English is the way it is; and presenting ideas and information on how teachers can effectively support children in developing a strong vocabulary and good spelling skills.

Here are some questions that might be useful to your practice and development. The first half are reflective, the second half have definite answers (you'll find them all in this book).

Reflective questions for professional development

● What are the main gaps in my own understanding of English?

● What is more important: a good vocabulary or good spelling skills?

● Do I understand the range of difficulties children might have with language acquisition and use?

● Does our school teach children the *metalanguage* of vocabulary and spelling?

- Are spelling lists effective?

- Which spelling rules are good, and which are misleading?

- What is the best way to assess spelling?

- How can I differentiate spelling programs for my class/school?

- How can I make good use of technology?

- Which children would benefit from targeted interventions?

- Are there suitable resources for supporting spelling and vocabulary in my classroom, and can the children I teach use them effectively?

- Should my classroom emphasis be on spoken or written vocabulary?

- Should my classroom emphasis be on formal or figurative language?

- Is my classroom 'language rich'?

- What would be the best strategy for developing children's vocabulary in my class/school?

Questions with straightforward answers

- Which languages is English derived from?

- What were the key factors that helped English become the accepted language of the UK?

- How many people in the world speak English?

- How many words are there in the English language?

- What percentage of English words are phonetic?

- How many new words do infant children acquire each day?

- What is the average active vocabulary of an adult?

- What is the average passive vocabulary of an adult?

- What percentage of the English language is phonetic?

- Does writing with a pen or pencil affect learning differently from using a keyboard?

- Is the percentage of language problems in UK prisons higher than in the UK at large?

- Can you name any famous dyslexics?

A brief history of the English language

Chapter 1

Here's a question you can't answer (but do have a go):

How many words are there in the English language?

This is not to cast aspersions on your knowledge or abilities –
it is a question that has no definite answer. Not only do different
dictionaries have different word counts, there is also debate over
whether acronyms (such as *OED*) and proper names (such as
London) should be added to the count. To go further, what about
English around the world? There are many words unique to
other English-speaking countries which frequently cross borders
as global communications become the norm. And there's more:
should we count historical words no longer used, regional words,
and the huge numbers of Latin-derived words for the flora and
fauna of the world?

Even if we could agree on these categories, the present will
scupper us. New words appear every day, which eventually find
their way into our daily language. English is ever-changing.

So, how did English evolve, and how did it become formalised
into the wide-ranging rules that govern its correct usage today?

A brief history of the English language

Subject facts

The words that you are reading now belong to a language that is a member of the Indo-European family of languages. Relatives (some rather distant!) of this family include Bengali, Portuguese, Russian, Spanish, French, German, Greek, Hindi, Punjabi and Urdu. The origins of this family of languages goes back to around 5000BC or earlier.

As people migrated and separated, new variations evolved and branched off: the Indo-Iranian languages; Hellenic (Greek); Celtic, and various others including Germanic. The first millennium BC saw the development of the Germanic languages in Northern Europe, from which current day German, Dutch and English are all descended.

The first steps towards the creation of English were taken when the Angles, Saxons and Jutes started migrating to Britain in the 5th century AD, occupying much of the Eastern and Central areas. History now refers to the period from around AD500 to 1066 as the Anglo-Saxon era, and refers to the language that developed as Anglo-Saxon, or Old English. Like those who first spoke it, this language had Western Germanic origins. Further influence came from Latin (due to the Roman legacy and spreading Christianity); Norse (from the invading Vikings), and Celtic (spoken by people on the fringes of the Anglo-Saxon territory, to the west).

The next big change came in 1066 with the arrival of the Normans. Although Anglo-Saxon did not die out as a language at once, the new ruling class spoke in Norman-French and Latin. The language that evolved over the next 400 years is now known as Middle English. In the early 15th century 'The Chancery Standard' became established as a standardised form of English for government use. It was based on the London and East Midland dialect, and the clerks that used it would have known French and Latin. It became established for most official use apart from within the church, which still used Latin.

The contribution of Latin to world languages is enormous. Vulgar Latin, spoken by soldiers and settlers, became the foundation for what are known as the *Romance languages* such as Spanish, French, Portuguese and Italian. Not only did Latin provide the foundations for the French language that was introduced to England in 1066, it also came with an alphabet.

The beginning of the Tudor era (1485) moved the language forward into Early Modern English. The key factors influencing this change were technology – the creation of the printing press – and religion – the creation of the Church of England. After Henry VIII broke away from the Catholic Church, the Bible was written in English along with the Book of Common Prayer, both of which were printed in significant numbers, helping English to begin to embed itself as the language of the nation. Despite this, there was still a significant variety of dialects around the country, and it was not until the 18th century, in the Georgian era, that Modern English came into being, with perhaps the pivotal moment being the creation of Dr Johnson's *Dictionary of the English Language* in 1755. Although there have been tweaks and changes ever since, this is the language we now use.

Samuel Johnson was an early lexicographer, a term which he drolly defined as *a writer of dictionaries; a harmless drudge, that busies himself in tracing the original, and detailing the signification of words.*

Why you need to know these facts

• Understanding the historical evolution of our language can help you to appreciate why it works the way it does. It can also be helpful for learning other languages (see page 18) and improve your knowledge of English history!

Vocabulary

Indo-European – a family of languages from around 5000BC in which English has its origins.
Lexicographer – a writer, editor or compiler of dictionaries.

A brief history of the English language

Linguistic – of or relating to language.
Middle English – the language that evolved in the Middle Ages after the Norman conquest.
Modern English – the language we now use, with its foundations in the Georgian era.
Old English – or Anglo-Saxon, derived from the Germanic languages of the Angles, Jutes and Saxons.
Romance languages – languages that have their origins in Latin.

Amazing facts

The closest living language to Latin is… Romanian.

Teaching ideas

● Find a selection of Old and Middle English words and have children guess and/or research their meanings. Some are easier than others! For example:

Modern English	Middle English	Old English
autumn	autumpne	hærfæst
child	child	bearn
five	five	fif
midnight	middel-night	middeneaht
person	person	mann
teacher	instructour	lareow
walk	walken	gan

The origins of words

Subject facts

Etymologists are concerned with the origins of words and their historical development. Their craft is known as etymology. An etymological dictionary, paper-based or online, will provide you with a great deal of information about word origins.

Let's return to the original question at the start of this chapter – *How many words are there in the English language?* Thinking of only the body of words that are used in everyday life in the United Kingdom, ignoring (for the moment) words coming from other English-speaking cultures, a trawl through a quality dictionary will reveal in excess of half a million words. And if that isn't enough, remember that new words (such as the verb *to text*) are constantly appearing. (A new word that is becoming more popular, but is not yet embedded into mainstream usage is called a *neologism*.)

And yet, despite everything that has happened to shape the English language over the past 1500 years, its core is still Anglo-Saxon. Of the 100 most frequently used words in English, 98 are Germanic in origin.

The 100 most frequent words in English

the	they	when	come
be	we	make	its
to	say	can	over
of	her	like	think
and	she	time	also
a	or	no	back
in	an	just	after
that	will	him	use

have	my	know	two
I	one	take	how
it	all	people	our
for	would	into	work
not	there	year	first
on	their	your	well
with	what	good	way
he	so	some	even
as	up	could	new
you	out	them	want
do	if	see	because
at	about	other	any
this	who	than	these
but	get	then	give
his	which	now	day
by	go	look	most
from	me	only	us

The majority of these 100 words are single-syllable words. The majority of the words in the list are function words as their role is to connect longer words to help create meaning. The other words are content words and these can be seen as more interesting to explore. The top ten of each of the following categories are generally short, and deal with the fundamentals of life, see the following table.

Nouns	Verbs	Adjectives
1 time	1 be	1 good
2 person	2 have	2 new
3 year	3 do	3 first
4 way	4 say	4 last
5 day	5 get	5 long
6 thing	6 make	6 great
7 man	7 go	7 little
8 world	8 know	8 own
9 life	9 take	9 other
10 hand	10 see	10 old

Across the whole of our language though, the proportions for word-origins are fairly evenly divided between Germanic and French/Latin, which has helped to give us a particularly rich vocabulary. Look at these words, and compare the short, Germanic words with the longer classical words.

Germanic	French	Latin
Fire	Flame	Conflagration
Fast	Firm	Secure
Ask	Question	Interrogate

A small percentage of our words come from Greek and other languages. Contributions from other languages are mainly more recent additions to the language (see page 20). Greek had influenced Latin long before it came to our shores, and provides the basis for many medical terms. In particular, Greek suffixes are easy to spot, such as '-phobia' from *phobos* – *fear*, giving us *claustrophobia*, *arachnophobia*, and so on.

Furthermore, we still have lots in common with other languages, as the chart below shows. The famous language teacher Michel Thomas would stress early in his lessons that to 'get by' in another language we only require a few thousand words, and, given that for some European languages the rules aren't massively different from our own, structuring the teaching correctly could result in rapid improvement for learners. One thing he pointed out was that some languages often have many words in common with English and, to a degree, these follow very consistent patterns. Look at these lists:

Suffix: '-tion'		
English	**French**	**Spanish**
attention	attention	atención
creation	création	creación
realisation	réalisation	realización

Suffix: '-able'		
English	**French**	**Spanish**
acceptable	acceptable	aceptable
reasonable	raisonnable	razonable
believable	croyable	creíble

Of course, it doesn't always work, as the last row shows (although *credible* is a close alternative), and the pronunciation (French: *prononciation*, Spanish: *pronunciación*) for each language has its own set of rules, but seeing links like this can help with learning a second language.

Finally, in considering how English came to be, the invention of print was very significant indeed. Not only was it a catalyst for rapidly increasing the availability of printed matter, it initiated the road to commonly accepted standards for English. Publications such as the King James Bible, and key writers such as William

Shakespeare, created new words and phrases that are still used today, such as *Money is the root of all evil*, *scapegoat*, *unearthly*, *vulnerable* and *well-bred*.

However, it's not just writers who create new words; technological innovation plays its part (*mouse* and *spam* both have additional meanings now), and they just seem to appear.

The written word has truly taken root. It is estimated that 25,000 novels were published in the UK in 2011, a staggering 68 novels per day. On top of that is the wide range of daily newspapers and periodicals, not to mention the vast new swathes of text appearing on websites and blogs, and in personal emails and texts. If the spoken word is your preference, as well as interpersonal communication, you have radio and television, pretty much 24/7. English has come of age, and we are immersed in it.

Why you need to know these facts

● The more you understand the language that we use, the more adept you can become at teaching it, and teaching with it. In addition, researching the origins of words (*etymology*) can be an interesting classroom activity for older primary children; both in its own right and combined with studying history.

Vocabulary

Etymology – the study of word origins.
Neologism – a word entering common discourse, but not yet embedded into mainstream use.

Amazing facts

Shakespeare contributed around 2000 new words to our language!

A brief history of the English language

Teaching ideas

- Turn the children into word detectives. Ensuring they are proficient in dictionary use (see Chapter 3), give them access to online or paper-based etymological dictionaries and create displays, such as timelines, or books showing the origins of words.

- Linking to Religious Education, The Lord's Prayer can be found in Old, Middle and Modern English translations. Comparing these side-by-side is an interesting insight into the evolution of English.

- The late, great Douglas Adams, author of *The Hitchhiker's Guide to the Galaxy*, also co-wrote a book called *The Meaning of Liff*. It is a humorous book that creates lots of new words for situations and items that may otherwise be undefined in the English language.

- There is lots of fun to be had in creating your own 'new words' with meanings, and creating dictionary-style entries for them.

Home and abroad – variations in English

Subject facts

Although English is now well established as our national language, there is still significant variation in its use across the UK. Travelling through the UK, it is quite extraordinary how it changes rapidly from one county to the next. The accent, features and idiosyncrasies of any one region's dialect often makes it relatively easy for people to identify a speaker's origin, wherever they might encounter them.

Colloquial English is a large body of words and phrases that are used informally by most people, such as *gonna* for 'going to', and *on tenterhooks* (meaning a state of uneasiness). The origins of phrases such as this are both interesting and useful; while they are informal, understanding and using them can help to broaden your vocabulary (see Chapter 8).

Standard English refers to English language that is considered 'correct', uninfluenced by regional dialect or colloquialisms. It is often linked to 'received pronunciation' or RP – the accepted, 'correct' way of speaking English. It is usual to hear standard English and RP spoken by newsreaders and politicians.

Over the last 300 or so years English has spread to many parts of the world, mainly due to explorers and colonial expansion. Its popularity has been sustained by the internet and extensive use in global business and other international communications. English is the third most-spoken language in the world (after Mandarin Chinese and Spanish). It has the status of an official language in over 70 countries, with over one-third of a billion people having it as their first language, and around twice that number able to speak it to some extent, as a foreign or second language. As such, further varieties of the language have evolved and developed their own unique attributes. Indeed, some of these, in particular American words and expressions, are now entering the everyday language of the UK and other countries. Words from non-English speaking countries occasionally enter our language too, particularly through food, such as *pizza*, *paella* and *bhaji*.

Why you need to know these facts

● Children in primary schools are required to engage with and create a wide range of text types. As such, it is important for them to be able to distinguish between casual and formal usage when considering their audience and in developing the tone of a piece of writing. In addition, learning about regional dialects and international usage is both important in understanding the children's own society and the everglobalising world they live in, as well as reinforcing their geographical understanding, both social and regional.

A brief history of the English language

Vocabulary

Dialect – the variation (from standard English) principally in grammar and vocabulary but also the pronunciation of a particular region.
Colloquialism – a word or phrase used in informal language.
Received pronunciation – the way standard English is spoken, without regional variation.
Standard English – the accepted 'correct' form of English.

Amazing facts

Over one billion people speak English as a first, second or foreign language.

Common misconceptions

There is a difference between English being a national language of a country, and it being an official language. For example, English is the *de facto* language only of the UK, America, Australia and New Zealand.

Teaching ideas

● Try to source audio/video files of people speaking English from different parts of the UK and the world, or team up with schools and swap audio files with them. Use this as a basis for discussing dialects and accents. Some TV and films are also useful for this if they are suitable for the primary setting.

● Create a collection of colloquialisms and slang, with accurate definitions and origins, adding them to a class book or display.

English in the digital age

Subject facts

The internet and mobile phones have also contributed enormously to the spread of English as a global language. It is also changing our writing and reading habits. Many people now type more than they write, read from a screen and not a printed page and chat using text rather than their voice.

Furthermore, texting creates the need to converse concisely. The sometimes fiddly nature of inputting text on mobile phones, and the rapid responses required, means that new forms of words are appearing, with acronyms, abbreviations and unusual spellings all becoming well established. This is known colloquially as 'SMS language' or 'textese'.

Cover the right-hand column with your hand. How many of these SMS words and phrases you know?

SMS	English
gr8	great
LOL	laugh out loud
HAND	have a nice day
2mrw	tomorrow
cu	see you
4	for
btw	by the way

Whether this is something to be alarmed about or to embrace is something of a debate, but it seems like it is here to stay. For those uneasy with such simplifications, there may be some consolation in knowing that software is becoming smarter and better at correcting our mistakes and predicting what we want to say

A brief history of the English language

Why you need to know these facts

- As mentioned earlier, English is ever-changing and ever-growing. An invention in human history as enormous as the internet is inevitably going to have an effect on our language. The speed at which this language has evolved, and is easily understood, means it cannot be ignored. Young people love technology and communicating – it is probably wise for adults and teachers to understand their language.

Vocabulary

SMS – short message service.
Textese – the language of texting (or SMS language).

Amazing facts

It has been estimated that over six trillion text messages were sent in 2010 – that's nearly 200,000 every second!

Resources

Language, the Basics by RL Trask (Routledge)
If you are interested in how English came to be and how it works, books by David Crystal aimed at the general public will serve you well. He is a well-respected linguist, who believes language must constantly evolve. His style is generally light and very accessible. Good ones to start with are listed below:
Words Words Words by David Crystal (OUP)
The Fight for English by David Crystal (OUP)
Begat: the King James Bible and the English Language by David Crystal (OUP)

Children and language

More than anything else, it is language that places humans apart from other species. Many species communicate using sounds, gestures and smells, but the complexity and variety of human languages is unique. That humans have created such a range of ever-evolving languages and dialects, and that knowing any one of these languages potentially allows us meaningful communication with any other human, anywhere in the world, is somewhat mind-boggling.

Humans have also created symbolic systems (usually text) for their languages and, along with the fact that we can *think* in language, this has facilitated the rapid growth and dissemination of knowledge and understanding that shapes our world today.

So, how do we do it? Many linguists and psychologists suggest that the innate ability to acquire language is hard-wired into our genes – we have evolved to be creatures of language.

Biological factors – nature

Subject facts

We can speak because of two things: our vocal tract and our brain.

The mechanics of speech

The vocal tract, in essence, consists of the larynx, or voice box, and the mouth; these combine to produce sounds. The image on page 26 shows a cross section of a human vocal tract, which differs significantly from those of other primates. We have a long trachea (windpipe) separated from the oesophagus (which takes food to the stomach) by the epiglottis.

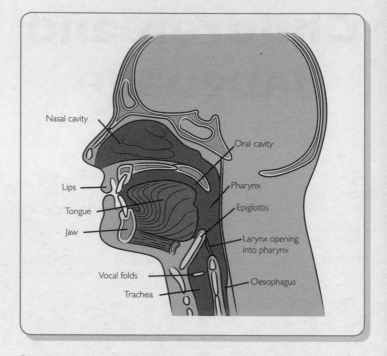

Sounds are created when the diaphragm forces air from the lungs up the trachea. The vocal folds (chords) then adjust to create different sounds as air moves through them, with the mouth then forming a complex range of positions involving the teeth, palate, tongue and lips to add further variation.

Our amazing brains

As well as controlling the vocal tract, the brain acquires language aurally, retains it, processes it, and uses the rules that surround its usage to create new and unique combinations of words.

In recent decades knowledge about how the brain is structured and functions has increased significantly. The brain consists of a dense, complex mass of billions of neurons connected by trillions (yes, *trillions*) of synapses. It is divided into two clear hemispheres, and language, particularly grammar, is processed and produced in the left hemisphere. Although there is much still to learn, psychologists and neurologists have identified key parts of the brain that contribute to language:

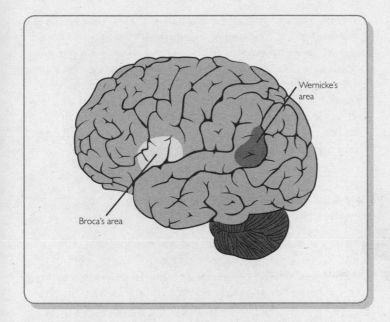

● **Broca's area:** Believed to be a key part of the brain used for speech production, where speech is planned in verbal short-term memory. It is also used for comprehending complex sentences.

● **Wernicke's area:** This part of the brain is thought to be used to connect the sounds of words with their written meaning. In other words, for understanding spoken and written language.

But don't be fooled – it isn't nearly so simple! Other parts of the brain seem to come into play at different times, and can even compensate for damaged areas.

From birth we are surrounded by language, and to survive we need to be able to communicate. So, we pick up language. Anecdotal evidence abounds to show how uniform the average human being is in this capacity. Children whose parents are from different continents and cultures to that which they are born and grow up in often speak with the fluency and intonation of a native. Equally, children who grow up in bilingual homes seem to pick up both languages effortlessly – a fact which is all the more amazing when each language contains sounds uncommon to the other.

The brain acquires language in two ways: it stores new words and it learns rules. It is the rules of a language that allow us to create our own, unique utterances. In young children we get a glimpse of the innate understanding of rules through their incorrect use of irregular verbs. Young children frequently say *buyed* instead of *bought* and *sayed* instead of *said,* showing the rule of adding '-ed' to the infinitive to form the past tense being applied. As time goes on and more and more correct language is processed, children generally correct these errors for themselves.

Why you need to know these facts

● Teaching is all about thought and communication – both in the teacher's daily interactions, and in the development of these attributes in the children they teach. There is a lot more to it, of course, but language underpins most of what goes on in schools. Understanding how language is generated can help you assess specific difficulties children might have and source appropriate help for them (see page 36).

Vocabulary

Broca's area – the part of the brain used for speech production.
Larynx – the voice box.
Vocal tract – the whole structure for making sounds: the larynx and the mouth.
Wernicke's area – the part of the brain used for understanding language.

Amazing facts

Polyglots are people who can speak several different languages. While true fluency is hard to measure, some people have claimed to be able to speak well over 20 different languages!

Environmental factors – nurture

Subject facts

We can all be said, at any particular time, to possess a vocabulary – a store of words in our brain. This store is ever changing – usually increasing – though not always. The average adult has a productive (or active) vocabulary of over 30,000 words, and a receptive (or passive) vocabulary of anything between 50,000 and 100,000.

Typical chronology of children's linguistic development	
0–3 months	Babies notice familiar voices. They cry to communicate pain and hunger.
3–6 months	Babies start to make a wider range of sounds – squeals, sighs, gurgles. They can watch speakers' mouths.
6–12 months	Babies can focus on those speaking to them. They enjoy 'cooing' and 'babbling', making a wider range of sounds, including recognisable phonemes. They may utter their first word or two.
1–2 years	Toddlers can make more complex sounds and use a small range of words, typically linked to their needs.
2–4 years	Pre-school children develop vocabulary at a rapid rate. Four-year-olds can have vocabularies of around 1000 words, which they use in simple sentences. They enjoy listening to stories and can retell the story's essence.

4–7 years	In the infant years children start to communicate fluently, with active vocabularies of 2000 words or more. They speak in longer, complex sentences and can readily retell and discuss stories, articulating most sounds correctly. They may still use some grammatical rules incorrectly, such as *buyed* for 'bought'. They start to acquire words at an astonishing rate, around ten new words per day, and they will build up receptive vocabularies of up to 20,000 words. Depending on the educational approach they encounter, they also start to read and write.
7–11 years	Children continue to develop their vocabulary and can achieve fluency in speaking, reading and writing. Their comprehension skills increase greatly, and as they move towards adolescence they effectively use inference and deduction, often with complex vocabularies and sentence structures. By the time they leave primary school, children will have receptive vocabularies of around 50,000 words.

The above chart provides an overview of the typical stages of language development. Yet, as many of us know, all children have different vocabularies and linguistic capabilities. This is in part due to the fact that they are different biologically, but it is also due to their life experiences and the environment in which they live. It is one of the most difficult aspects of a primary teacher's work, especially those working in Early Years, to have responsibility for children from a diverse range of home and social environments, where they will be having a wide range of experiences:

● **Language input:** the language that children hear, either directly spoken to them, or being used around them. As well as other people, this might include television, radio and recorded materials.

● **Interaction:** parents, other family members, friends, and perhaps nursery workers, will interact with babies and young children; talking to them, singing to them and playing games. As we all know, many adults (as well as the children) derive a huge amount of pleasure from such interaction.

● **Active cultivation:** this sort of activity is different from the interaction just mentioned, in that it is done with the focused intention of *trying* to improve the young child's linguistic capabilities. Not everyone agrees that this is a good idea, preferring lots of normal everyday interaction, though most would agree that it is better than nothing.

Clearly the quality of these experiences will vary for each child. In a shocking report in 2008 – *Getting in Early: Primary Schools and Early Intervention* – it was estimated that one in ten children start school unable to talk in sentences, rising to 50 per cent in some parts of the country. It has also been suggested that some children starting school at five are already two years behind the average.

Why you need to know these facts

● The astonishing rate at which children acquire language, and the huge variety in quality of pre-school experiences and development they have had provides schools with a critical role in accurately assessing children and planning their curriculum accordingly. All primary schools need to have the knowledge, structures and resources to do this effectively.

Vocabulary

Productive (or active) vocabulary – words actively used.
Receptive (or passive) vocabulary – words that we know but don't use in everyday communication.

Amazing facts

Pre-school children in language-rich environments may hear ten million or more spoken words per year. Those in language-deprived environments may hear as little as two million.

Common misconceptions

Tabloid newspapers might not be everybody's cup of tea, but a frequently stated myth is that to understand them we only require the reading age of an eight-year-old. The linguist David Crystal estimates that a typical edition of *The Sun* newspaper has a vocabulary of around 6000 different words (in his test he found *embezzle*, *enigmatically* and *entrant* among many others). To put that into context, the King James Bible contains a vocabulary of 8000 different words.

Language and learning

Subject facts

In all aspects of life we often use language to help ourselves to learn (though not always, such as musical learning). There are many theories of learning, the best known of which demonstrate the educational spectrum: Skinner, Piaget and Vygotsky.

- **Skinner:** As a behaviourist, Skinner viewed language use as a behaviour, its development being 'encouraged' by positive reinforcement from the child's environment (including those within it).

- **Piaget:** Known to most teachers from their training days, Piaget developed a theory consisting of stages of development which were prerequisites for learning. He believed that children construct knowledge based on interaction with the new artefacts and experiences (including taught material). As such, he saw language as supporting, and secondary to, cognition (though this was not to deny its importance).

- **Vygotsky:** In contrast to Piaget, Vygotsky viewed this more-or-less the other way around. He suggested that learning precedes development and, as such, is very much a social thing. He regarded language as critical to thought, suggesting that the speaking/writing of words was not the result of a thought, but that the words *complete* the thought.

Who was right? All the theories have value, but whichever one an educational establishment leans towards to inform its own pedagogy – formal or informal; progressive or traditional; child-centred or teacher-led; skills-based or knowledge-based – we should all agree that being literate is essential for successful learning and development. Once children move on to secondary school they will be immersed in language for several hours a day, usually coming from subject specialists, each with their own lexicon of words relevant to their subject. Any deficit in linguistic development can affect learning across the entire curriculum.

Although the traditional emphasis in schools as been on literacy – reading and writing – the importance of children's aural (hearing) and oral (speaking) development should not be underestimated. Even as children develop their reading and writing skills, teachers should be ever mindful of the benefits of high quality speaking-and-listening activities in extending children's linguistic development.

Why you need to know these facts

● Primary school teachers have the complex job of helping children to develop their linguistic abilities alongside their intellects, with language often used to stimulate thought and assess understanding. Developing your understanding of how language can support intellectual development and learning in other subjects can help to focus your teaching techniques and classroom practice.

Vocabulary

Aural – of or relating to the sense of hearing.
Lexicon – the vocabulary of a particular language.
Oral – of or related to speaking.
Pedagogy – The method and practice (or art) of teaching.

Handy tips

Thinking out loud, or 'verbalising', can be very effective for raising your understanding and awareness of knowledge and situations. Try this exercise the next time you drive (or if you don't drive it can work when walking too). As you move down a street describe out loud everything that is happening that will affect your actions in the immediate future, for example, *parked car on the left, pedestrian looks like she is going to cross, traffic lights ahead…* and so on. Try this same idea with children in the classroom – not to explain how they have done something, but to verbalise their thoughts while they are doing something.

Moving on to the printed word

Subject facts

Just as children instinctively pick up language aurally then start using it verbally, they will show an increasing awareness that text exists, and that people use this text in all sorts of ways.

Reading and writing are two very different skills. Reading, in essence, is about memory – developing a knowledge of the sounds that letters and letter combinations represent, and gradually understanding the rules that govern their usage. Writing, however, involves recalling those words and then controlling the hand to reproduce them.

As with speaking, we go through various stages in learning to read and write. There is some debate as to whether a rich, immersive environment can aid strong development in reading and writing skills the way it can in oracy, or whether a more structured curriculum is more appropriate. Both have their strengths and weaknesses, and both – to greater or lesser degrees – are the mainstay of literacy lessons in the UK. Typically, in their time at primary school, children will experience and produce a wide range of text types and, by the age of 11, they can be capable of reading large, quite complex novels and writing extended fiction and non-fiction pieces with increasing accuracy and style.

The current bedrock that underpins this development is the teaching of phonics. There are two basic approaches to phonics – synthetic and analytic, with the former very much in favour in UK schooling at present. So what's the difference?

Synthetic phonics, where children are systematically and discreetly taught the 44 sounds (phonemes) of the English language, and the letter (grapheme) combinations that create these sounds. The use of meaningful texts for the teaching of letter-sound combinations is less important in synthetic phonics, although this should not be interpreted as undervaluing the use of suitable texts. Following considerable, well-publicised success, synthetic phonics is currently very popular, though some critics have concerns that, applied too much in isolation, it can demoralise children with speech and language difficulties, as well as having the potential to undermine the motivation and wider benefits of reading.

Analytic phonics, which adopts a whole-word approach to learning to read, helps children to read words by breaking them down into their constituent sounds such as *d-o-g* and *sh-ou-t*, when they need to. It is usually based around meaningful texts, and encourages children to use contextual clues to decipher words – the place in the text, the words around them, and picture clues. Critics argue that its weakness lies in the assumption that all children already have sufficient phonetic knowledge to do this.

Why you need to know these facts

● Understanding the ways in which reading and writing develop and their impact on children's general language development can help you to structure lessons more appropriately, assess published materials for their suitability, and carefully model your own use of language in the classroom.

Vocabulary

Analytic phonics – an approach to phonics in which the phonemes associated with particular graphemes are not pronounced in isolation.

Grapheme – the visual representation of sound, usually in letters.

Oracy – the ability to clearly speak and understand spoken language.

Phoneme – the smallest identifiable sound in a language.

Synthetic phonics – an approach to reading based on pronouncing sounds in isolation and blending them together to construct words. For writing the words are segmented into phonemes and in turn the related graphemes.

Amazing facts

Roughly 85 per cent of the English language is phonetically decodable. Unfortunately, the 15 per cent that is irregular contains many high-frequency words.

Specific difficulties

Subject facts

Looking back through this chapter it is easy to appreciate why spelling is so difficult:

- We are born into environments with differing degrees of language-richness.
- We must then learn the graphical representation of our language, which in the case of English is diverse and not entirely regular.
- Finally, we must also learn to control one of our hands to reproduce those words.

If becoming proficient in literacy is a long and complicated road for all of us, imagine how it must be for those with specific problems, for whom our hotchpotch language really is a barrier. Due to the complex nature of our sound-letter relationships, children with difficulties are at a distinct disadvantage compared to those in countries with truly phonetic systems, such as Italy. This isn't to say that conditions such as dyslexia do not exist in such countries, but children do tend to cope better there.

The following list is an overview of the most common difficulties affecting language development that may be encountered in mainstream schools.

● **Aphasia** (from Greek: *speechlessness*) is a language disorder resulting from brain trauma or, in older people, changes resulting from tumours in the brain, infections or dementia. Typically, people have difficulty remembering words, but in more extreme cases people lose the ability to read and write.

● **Asperger's syndrome** is a lifelong condition that affects, to differing degrees, individuals' abilities in social interaction and communication. It is increasingly considered to be part of the autistic spectrum, at the lower end.

● **Autism** is a brain disorder that affects people's ability to relate to the external world. Typical problems include difficulties in verbal and non-verbal communication. Language difficulties in children with autism vary greatly, from being unable to speak, to having rich and productive vocabularies, although they can often struggle to use language effectively or appropriately.

● **Blindness and visual impairment** creates a range of problems for language acquisition, as visual clues and context are often missing. For children with severe sight problems, specialist educational environments are usually required.

● **Cerebral palsy** describes a varying range of physical disabilities caused by damage to the brain during pregnancy, childbirth, or infancy. It can affect the muscles that control speech, resulting in problems with pronunciation (*dysarthria*, see overleaf), as well as fine and gross motor control.

● **Deafness** can exist in varying degrees and may change over children's lives. Fully or partially hearing-impaired children are at a disadvantage in acquiring language and moving on to reading and writing, and often require specialist environments and/or intervention programmes.

- **Dysarthria** (from Greek: *bad-articulate*) is a problem with pronunciation due to damage to areas of the brain. This might be a symptom of cerebral palsy, but can also be caused by a range of trauma, illnesses and diseases. People with dysarthria often struggle to make themselves understood, and require intensive speech therapy with lots of on going practice.

- **Dysgraphia** (from Greek: *bad-draw*) is a specific difficulty with writing, which, as such, only becomes evident when children start learning to write. It may accompany other difficulties, but can exist regardless of how well a person may read or their general linguistic capabilities. Its origins can be in dyslexia, but issues with motor control and spatial skills can also be a cause.

- **Dyslexia** (from Greek: *bad-words*) is a learning difficulty that inhibits the ability to learn to read and write. It stems from having one or more of poor visual, auditory or spatial memory/abilities. A range of tests have been devised to diagnose dyslexia, although many people remain concerned that being *dyslexic* is a label too easily applied. The British Dyslexia Association suggests that ten per cent of the British population is dyslexic, four per cent severely so. It is generally recognised that early difficulties with phonics acquisition can be an indicator of dyslexia.

- **Dyspraxia** (from Greek: *bad-doing*) is a chronic neurological condition that affects coordination and movement control, as the brain fails to transmit messages to the body effectively. Dyspraxia can overlap with other conditions, such as dyslexia, and some studies suggest that up to half of all people with dyspraxia also may have Attention Deficit Hyperactivity Disorder (ADHD), although this remains a matter of considerable contention.

- **Mutism and elective mutism** are two very different conditions. Mute children have brain damage, and typically will have significant language problems. By contrast, elective mutism is a psychological disorder related to social anxiety. It is harder to assess, and may not be especially detrimental to language development, although intervening to address the underlying causes is of primary importance.

● **Language deprivation** is an environmental, rather than medical term, used to describe situations where children have been living in environments with minimal linguistic input. Typically, children from language-deprived environments have poor language skills, which vary according to the severity and duration of their experiences.

Why you need to know these facts

● Working in primary education will inevitably bring you in to contact with children who have problems with language. Identifying and addressing these problems early is very important. While your daily work may not require you to be an expert in specific language difficulties, understanding the essence and implications of the main range of language difficulties for children can help you to appreciate their difficulties; seek appropriate support; and feel comfortable when meeting with experts and carers to discuss specific children's needs.

Vocabulary

Aphasia – a language disorder resulting from brain trauma or disease.
Asperger's syndrome – a condition that affects social communication and interaction skills.
Autism – a brain disorder that affects perception of and response to the external environment.
Cerebral palsy – difficulties with motor control affecting different parts of the body.
Deafness – problems with hearing that may be partial or total.
Dysarthria – specific problems with clear articulation of words.
Dysgraphia – a specific difficulty with writing.
Dyslexia – a learning difficulty that inhibits the ability to learn to read and write.

Dyspraxia – a neurological condition that affects coordination and movement control.

Language deprivation – existing in an environment with minimal linguistic stimulation.

Mutism – being unable or unwilling to speak.

Common misconceptions

It is true to state that the average literacy level of prisoners is much lower than that of the general public, but a frequent mistake is to make a simple link between criminality and illiteracy. The reality is obviously much more complex – illiteracy is also a product of social and economic factors that may contribute to crime.

Resources

How to Identify and Support Children with Speech and Language Difficulties by Jane Speake (LDA)

Words and Rules by Steven Pinker (Weidenfeld & Nicolson) is an academic writing for the public at large. Interesting if you want to get to the heart of things.

Chapter 3

Dictionaries, thesauruses and technology

These tools, which support spelling and vocabulary development, are presented here so that you might consider their use as you read subsequent chapters. None of them provide the solution to effective learning, but as additional tools they are very useful and powerful. As children move through primary school they should become increasingly aware of, and exposed to, dictionaries, thesauruses and technology. It is possible that their first encounter with a dictionary and thesaurus will be in the classroom and, as such, it is worth spending time ensuring that children can use these effectively. We must also pay close heed to technology, which has rapidly grown to support writing in various ways that are impressive, but not always helpful to the young learner.

What is a dictionary?

Subject facts

The *Oxford English Dictionary* is considered by many to be the gold standard for English dictionaries. It is available in a range of versions, as well as online. Its definition of the word *dictionary* is as follows:

> dictionary > n. (pl. dictionaries) a book that lists the words of a language in alphabetical order and gives their meaning, or their equivalent in a different language.

Dr Samuel Johnson wrote the first comprehensive dictionary of English. His *Dictionary of the English Language* took nine years to write and was published in 1755. Prior to this, dictionaries had existed, but none were in any way comprehensive. Dr Johnson's book contained definitions for just under 43,000 words, as well as the innovation of illustrating some words using quotes from famous texts of the time, such as Shakespeare.

The rest, as they say, is history. Look in any good bookshop today and you will see a vast range of dictionaries of all shapes and sizes. There are dictionaries for words, slang, proverbs, computing, law, medicine, bilingual dictionaries and, of course, children's dictionaries.

Types of dictionary

It is important to select the appropriate dictionary according to how it will be used, and there are several types available:

- picture dictionaries
- first dictionaries
- illustrated dictionaries
- concise dictionaries
- pocket dictionaries
- spelling dictionaries
- phonetic dictionaries.

● **Picture dictionaries:** Aimed at introducing young children to the concepts of text and first words. Typically they are large, and have illustrated or photographic scenes with word labels dotted around them, or pictures of everyday objects with their words next to them. They will probably contain 100–200 words.

● **First dictionaries:** Usually contain illustrations, but their focus is more on words and their meanings. Useful for around age five and above, they contain around 1000–2000 words.

● **Illustrated dictionaries:** These can vary in size and length, and may vary in the number of illustrations. Some provide a picture for every word.

● **Junior and primary dictionaries:** Devised specifically for schools' use from age seven onwards, with anything between 5000–30,000 words.

- **Pocket dictionaries:** These are portable and easy to use. They may contain as many words as larger dictionaries, but with less information surrounding each word.

- **Concise dictionaries:** Perhaps the best known of all dictionaries. As the name suggests they provide brief, clear definitions to words, although they can still run to thousands of pages if they are covering most of the language. As such, they are probably not best suited to use in the primary classroom.

- **Spelling dictionaries:** These carry as many words as other dictionaries, but with much shorter definitions and minimal other information. This allows users to rapidly search for the correct spellings.

- **Phonetic dictionaries:** Different to most dictionaries, and need to be used carefully. Some arrange words according to their phonetic pronunciation, with the correct spelling given afterwards. One specific dictionary worth a mention is the *ACE spelling dictionary* published by LDA, which covers over 3000 key words arranged according to short vowels, long vowels and vowel sounds.

Why you need to know these facts

- From choosing dictionaries for whole-class use, to selecting books for specific individual needs, understanding the range of dictionaries and the information and support that they provide is crucial in effectively supporting learners' needs.

Amazing facts

The verb *set*, with over 430 senses consisting of approximately 60,000 words or 326,000 characters, is the longest entry in the *Oxford English Dictionary*.

Handy tips

If your school is thinking of ordering new dictionaries, try to trial some samples with some children. Not many children will want to use dictionaries for long periods of time, so you need to decide which ones will best suit their needs. Is your main focus checking spellings or increasing the children's understanding of precise meanings, or is grammar or phonetic pronunciation important to you? In particular, be sure to read the opening pages which will explain how the book is structured.

Using a dictionary

Subject facts

First and foremost, it is important for teachers and children to realise that possessing a dictionary is not the solution to instant improvement of spelling or vocabulary skills. Dictionary use requires a range of skills to guarantee successful word research. These include:

- knowing alphabetical order
- deducing word beginnings
- understanding syllables
- scanning
- interpreting entries.

● **Knowing alphabetical order** is an obvious requirement, but sometimes can still be insecure in children aged seven and above, and using it for second and third letters in a word can be tricky. Knowing the alphabet well immediately helps us to gauge roughly where to open the dictionary. Once the correct letter is located, dictionaries usually have *guide words* at the top of each page, typically next to the page number. The word at the top of the left-hand page is the first word on that page; the word at the top of the right-hand page being the very last word on that page. As such, these two words represent the range of words on that double-page spread, and children need practice in thumbing through dictionaries, looking only at these guide words to locate the pages that their word should be on.

- **Deducing word beginnings** where there are multiple grapheme-phoneme correspondences will require spelling skills, or at very least the ability to think through alternative possibilities. Children will then need to be able to apply their knowledge of the alphabet to the first, then second letter of the word, and so on. Appropriate support, such as phoneme-grapheme charts and high-frequency word lists, should also be available to the children.

- **Understanding syllables** is helpful in allowing children to focus on any one section of a word at a time.

- **Scanning** is typically considered a higher-order skill, and certainly as children near the end of their primary phase they should have had plenty of practice with this essential skill. Strong scanning skills will allow them to find words more efficiently.

- **Interpreting entries** requires good comprehension skills. Some dictionaries will give large swathes of information, only some of which may be useful; whereas small dictionaries may be too concise for users looking for detailed information.

It is a mistake to assume that once the word is found the rest of the work is plain sailing. Once a word is located, the information encountered depends very much on the type of dictionary, and the information for any one word may include:
- the correct spelling of the word, called the *headword*
- the phonetic pronunciation of the word
- the class of the word, for example, *noun*, *adjective* or just *n.*, *adj.* (note that word classes are sometimes called parts of speech (see page 66))
- one or more definitions of the word
- cross-references to other words, usually synonyms
- irregular or confusing forms
- words from the same family (sometimes called derivatives)
- compound words derived from the main word
- idioms and phrases incorporating the word
- notes on usage

- notes on the word's etymological origins, such as where it came from.

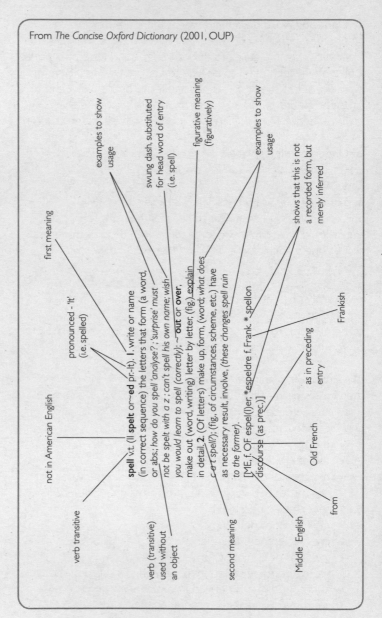

From *The Concise Oxford Dictionary* (2001, OUP)

Why you need to know these facts

● As children move through primary school it is possible to construct an effective progression of dictionary skills alongside the school's long-term plans for literacy. Dictionary usage is much more than finding the correct spelling for a word. It involves a complex range of skills which, used effectively, can contribute to children's literary development, helping them to understand their language more fully and empowering them to communicate clearly and effectively.

Vocabulary

Guide words – the words at the top of each page in a dictionary that allow us to see the range of words on that double-page spread.
Headword – the word under which a dictionary entry is listed.

Common misconceptions

The word *concise* suggests brevity. In fact, concise dictionaries are often weighty books with thousands of pages. They are concise in that they offer an alternative to the multi-volume complete dictionaries typically found in libraries.

Handy tips

Remember to plan explicit lessons on dictionary skills relative to children's ages that will allow them to use these skills independently in their work. Encourage this by having a good supply of dictionaries to hand in the classroom. Chapter 8 contains further advice.

Teaching ideas

● Set up a time trial to assess the children's understanding of alphabetical order. Give the children a list of 20 words, researched in advance, that you know will occur as *guide words* in the dictionaries they are using. They must find each word and write down which page it is on. Time how long it takes them to find all the words. (You may find it beneficial to focus on words all beginning with the same letter in some exercises, to allow the children to see how alphabetical order is used for the subsequent letters too.)

● To develop familiarity and scanning skills, working from a prepared list, dictate individual words to the class and ask them to locate each word in their dictionaries. Start with easy words, moving on to alternative grapheme-phoneme correspondences or irregular words as you see fit. Continue this exercise by moving on to longer, multisyllabic words.

● Choose words that may be new to the children in your class, perhaps via a new topic you are exploring, and ask them to research and interpret the words' meanings. Alternatively, give children sentences with a more complex vocabulary than they are used to. Can they deduce the meaning of the text using their dictionaries to help them?

Using a thesaurus

Subject facts

A thesaurus is an index of selected words and their synonyms (words that have a similar meaning). Some thesauruses will also include antonyms (words of an opposite meaning) and related words. Unlike dictionaries, they do not provide in-depth definitions of words, though they may provide a brief explanation and examples of use. Thesauruses for schools are available in illustrated and age-appropriate formats. Typically, they will contain around the same number of words as their age-equivalent dictionary.

The first well-known thesaurus of English was published in 1852. Called *Roget's Thesaurus* after its creator, Peter Roget, this thesaurus was originally organised into themes. Thematic thesauruses are still available today, although those with alphabetical listings are generally favoured in schools.

Let's see the *Oxford Thesaurus of English* entry for *thesaurus*:

Thesaurus, noun
= wordfinder, wordbook, synonym dictionary/lexicon;
rare synonymy

We can see that many of the skills needed for dictionary work apply equally to a thesaurus. As with dictionaries, people may use thesauruses to check spellings of known words, but the main purpose is to enrich vocabulary and make writing more varied. As such, they need to be used with care and caution – it certainly isn't simply a case of swapping words. Synonyms often have small nuances in meaning that differentiate them from each other, and, more importantly, we need to understand the everyday conventions for how words are used in context. For example, you might want to improve the sentence *Bob had a nice haircut*, and 'nice', as we know, is something of a bland word. However, blindly following our thesaurus could give us *Bob had a pleasant haircut*, or even *Bob had an enjoyable haircut*. Both sound wrong (even though they are grammatically correct), whereas *great* or *attractive* would both fit comfortably into the sentence.

Why you need to know these facts

- The thesaurus is a useful tool in schools' approaches to building children's literacy. In particular they can help to enrich writing and broaden vocabulary, providing they are used with care and attention.

Dictionaries, thesauruses and technology

Amazing facts

Dr Roget first wrote his thesaurus in 1805, but it was nearly 50 years before it was published.

Common misconceptions

Illustrated thesauruses (and indeed dictionaries) sometimes contain little more than one or two images per page; they do not necessarily provide pictures for every word. While they can include colours that may help some, their value can be relatively superficial.

Handy tips

Some publishers have also created combined dictionaries and thesauruses in one book. Once children's referencing skills have been established they may find a combined book more usable.

Teaching ideas

● Many of the teaching ideas presented for dictionary use can also be applied to learning to use a thesaurus. It is probably wise to hone these skills with a dictionary, and then focus thesaurus work on understanding nuances of meaning, as well as the rhythm and tone of language. Present children with individual sentences or whole poems and passages and ask them to improve it using a thesaurus. Selecting appropriate synonyms is very much a case of knowing what style you want to present, depending on genre and audience, and it will obviously take time to help children appreciate these subtleties.

Information technology

Subject facts

Technology, being the ubiquitous thing it has become, is more likely to have entered children's lives outside of school than dictionaries or thesauruses, and will influence their language. Mobile phones almost always come with predictive texting as standard (for good or bad); word processors and email packages have auto-correction and in-built dictionaries and thesauruses; and the internet is awash with online dictionaries and thesauruses of varying degrees of quality.

Hand-held electronic spell-checkers are relatively affordable, and spelling apps for smart-phones are available. Add to this the possibility of high-quality, affordable 'speech to text' software, and we are forced to accept that the way text is generated, and the speed of this generation, is no longer limited to how fast we can use a pen or type.

A wide range of child-focused software is also available, from simple animated alphabets and word recognition games to structured spelling practice and monitoring of performance, and more complex programs for helping children to write with words and symbols.

Why you need to know these facts

● That technology is of value in learning is undisputed, depending on how it is used. For example, children with significant handwriting problems can still demonstrate their linguistic capabilities, and teachers can facilitate engaging practice with suitable spelling programmes. But for children developing their literacy abilities, these technological advances are not necessarily a positive. There is no doubt that technology can help, especially for those with specific difficulties, but as with any tool its functionality and limitations need to be understood and assessed, not taken for granted. As such, technology's potential to support writing is something teachers must engage with.

● Nevertheless, it is essential that children fully understand about physical dictionaries and thesauruses, how they are structured and how to use them effectively before they encounter their digital counterparts. And, once children do start using digital equivalents, teachers need to be aware of their capabilities.

Vocabulary

Predictive text – a device's ability to 'guess' what word you are trying to type and to complete it or offer a range of options.

Speech to text software – allows users to dictate while the software converts their voice to text. Usually the software has to be 'trained' to recognise the idiosyncrasies of each person's voice. Currently this software is expensive for schools, mainly because it requires high-performance computers to work effectively.

Spell-checker – a portable electronic device, with a miniature keyboard, that allows users to check spellings. Advanced versions may include definitions and synonyms.

Common misconceptions

Many people still think that word processors usually provide American English spellings. Although this has been the case in the past, most word processors now come with both American and English spellings, as well as the facility to add your own words to the inbuilt dictionary.

If you are not yet convinced of the power of software, have a look at some of the 'visual thesauruses' available online. They create dynamic links between synonyms, including metaphoric meanings, as in the screenshot below, which resulted from entering the word *eat*. Users can then click on any one of the synonyms and move to new sets of links, as well as listen to the pronunciation and find out meanings.

As with all technology, once we have accepted its capabilities, we need to scrutinise its potential. For example, a different online thesaurus to the one shown on the right created quite a different word web.

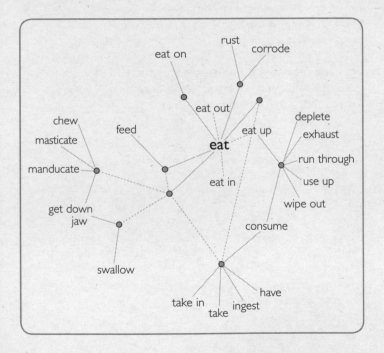

Resources

Ace spelling dictionary by David Moseley (LDA) is an aurally coded dictionary based on initial vowel sounds in words. Very useful for some children with specific spelling difficulties.

Educational publishers provide wide ranges of general, age-specific and focused dictionaries and thesauruses. Browsing their brochures will give you a good feel for what will best suit your school.

The Oxford Dictionary of English (OUP)
Collins English Dictionary (Collins)
The Chambers Dictionary (Chambers)
Cambridge School Dictionary (Cambridge University Press)
The Oxford Thesaurus of English (OUP)
Collins Thesaurus of the English Language (Collins)
Roget's Thesaurus of English Words and Phrases (Penguin)

They also provide good online services, some free:
Collins: http://www.collinsdictionary.com
OUP: http://oxforddictionaries.com/

Understanding words

Everything you'll ever say or write will be a collection of words. They come in all shapes and forms, and as we've already seen, from many different sources. The aim of this chapter is to provide you with a solid understanding of the anatomy of words: how they are composed, their different types, and the rules and irregularities that govern their construction.

Letters and sounds

Subject facts

Let's 'do the numbers':

- 26 letters (5 vowels and 21 consonants), all available in upper- and lower- case
- approximately 44 sounds
- over 500,000 words
- infinite combinations of words to communicate and make meaning for a lifetime, during which we will hear, speak, read and write many millions of them.

Put like that, it makes sense for children and teachers to have a good understanding of letters and sounds – the basics of their language. The smallest unit of sound is a *phoneme*, and there are approximately 44 of these in the English language. The written representation of a sound is called a *grapheme*: in English these are the 26 letters of the alphabet, and individually or combined they are used to represent the phonemes. This gives rise to the three key difficulties with the English alphabet system:

- A phoneme can be represented by between one and four letters.
- Some phonemes can be represented by more than one grapheme.
- Some graphemes can make more than one phoneme (the worst culprit being the 'ough' combination).

Grapheme/phoneme chart

Consonant phonemes and short-vowel phonemes			
Phoneme	Common spellings	Phoneme	Common spellings
/s/	sun, mouse, city, mess, science	/f/	fish, photo, coffee
/a/	apple	/l/	leg, spell
/t/	tap, better	/h/	hat
/p/	paper, hippo	/sh/	ship, mission, chef
/i/	ink, bucket	/z/	zebra, please, is, fizzy, sneeze
/n/	noise, knife, gnat	/w/	water, wheel, queen
/e/	egg, bread	/ch/	chip, watch
/d/	dog, puddle	/j/	jug, judge, giant, barge
/m/	man, hammer, comb	/v/	van, drive
/g/	game, egg	/y/	yes
/o/	octopus, want	/th/	thin
/c/ /k/	luck, cat, Chris, king, queen	/th/	then
/u/	umbrella, love	/ng/	ring, sink
/r/	rabbit, wrong, berry	/zh/	treasure
/b/	baby, cabbage		

Long-vowel phonemes			
Phoneme	Common spellings	Phoneme	Common spellings
/ai/	play, take, snail, baby	/ur/	burn, girl, term, heard, work
/ee/	feel, heat, me, pony	/au/	sauce, horn, door, warn, claw, ball
/igh/	tie, fight, my, bike, tiger	/ar/	car
/oa/	float, slow, stone, nose	/air/	hair, bear, share
/oo/	book, could, put	/ear/	ear, here, deer
/oo/	moon, clue, grew, tune	/ure/	sure, tour
/ow/	cow, shout	/ə/	teacher, collar, doctor, wooden, circus
/oi/	coin, boy		

The five vowels play a crucial role in the tone of our language, and as such they have a lot of work to do. There are short and long sounds for all of them. Look at the first letter in each of these word pairs and think about the sound it represents: *at/ate; every/even; in/ice; on/open; up/use*. We will come to some of the rules governing these variations later on (see page 76–77).

Where one grapheme consists of two letters to make a single sound, such as 'ch' in *chat*, it is called a 'digraph'. If two vowels combine to make a phoneme they are called a 'vowel digraph', such as 'ea' in *head*. However, if two different vowel sounds occur in the same syllable, such as /ai/ in *hay* which consists of /a/ and /i/ qualities, this is called a 'diphthong'. Similarly, the combination of two consonant sounds, such as 'gr' in *green* is called a 'blend'. Blends can also be created with digraphs such as 'thr' in *throw*, and with three consonant sounds such as 'str' in *strong*.

We must also remember the important role of 'syllables'. Syllables influence the rhythm of English. Typically, syllables have a vowel sound as their focus. *Dog* has one syllable – it is 'monosyllabic'. *Hamster* has two syllables (ham/ster), and like all words with more than one syllable it is 'polysyllabic'. Syllables can be very helpful for breaking down spellings (see Chapter 6).

A monosyllabic word only has one syllable. The most frequent monosyllabic words are CVC words which, as their acronym suggests, consist of a **c**onsonant, **v**owel and a final **c**onsonant. They are particularly beneficial for introducing children to letter sounds and spellings, as the letters always make their sounds as defined in the phonetic alphabet.

Monosyllabic words can be split into two parts – the onset and the rime – which are smaller than syllables, but can be bigger than phonemes. The onset is the initial consonant sound, such as '**c**-*at*' or '**sh**-*op*', and the rime is the vowel sound and the remainder of the syllable. This method is particularly useful for helping children with letter and blend sounds, and is typically practised with rhyming words.

We often pronounce words according to their syllables, but not always. The way we break down words is known as 'segmentation', and certain words lend themselves to being segmented differently, such as *sau-sa-ges* or *saus-a-ges*. The 'rules' surrounding this are relatively straightforward: we don't split digraphs, diphthongs or blends, and blends are usually pronounced in a group around the stressed vowel sound in the word, such as re-**sp**o̱nse. (Words always have one main stress in them, and this is always centred around a vowel.)

Capital letters also merit a mention. Although their main function is to aid clarity, for young learners they are another set of graphemes to be learned, and teachers need to carefully differentiate between letter names and sounds when introducing them.

Why you need to know these facts

● For most infant teachers the previous summary is nothing more than their daily bread and butter, but for some primary teachers who rarely work with infants they are much less common in daily classroom life. Understanding these facts can help with your approach to teaching English, as well as devising appropriate spelling programmes and diagnosing specific difficulties.

Vocabulary

Blend – bringing two sounds together in a smooth flow.
Digraph – a combination of two graphemes that represent a single sound.
Diphthong – a phoneme consisting of two vowels that are next to each other, where the sound starts with the first vowel and moves into the next.
Grapheme – the visual representation of sound, usually in letters.
Monosyllabic – a word with only one syllable.
Onset and rime – splitting monosyllabic words into an initial consonant sound and a final vowel-based sound.
Polysyllabic – a word with more than one syllable.
Segmentation – the act of dividing or partitioning words when speaking.
Syllable – a unit of pronunciation.
Vowel digraph – a combination of two vowel graphemes to represent a single sound.

Amazing facts

The poem at the start of this book uses the various pronunciations of 'ough' to good effect. In fact, there are at least eight ways to pronounce 'ough': *cough, hiccough, lough, plough, rough, though, through* and *thorough*!

Common misconceptions

Letter blends are not the same as digraphs. Digraphs create a unique sound, such as 'th', whereas blends bring two or more sounds together, such as 'bl' or 'thr'.

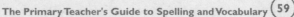

Handy tips

Use the 'metalanguage'. Metalanguage is the term used to explain a language. In this case 'blend', 'phoneme', and so on. Don't be afraid of using these terms with the children. They will pick them up easily enough, and it helps to demystify the learning.

Teaching ideas

● Create themed alphabet displays, showing the variety of sounds that apply to each grapheme.

● Play clapping games to help reinforce syllables, starting with simple words or children's names, moving on to longer words and even whole rhymes or songs. Alliteration and rhyme are excellent ways to reinforce sound patterns. Professor Usha Goswami has developed research and resources for many years based on rhyme, analogy and rhythm.

● Phonics isn't just for infants. Once in a while recap the essence of the alphabet and its complex uses, keeping children aware of the basics. Have a 'word of the day' appropriate to the children's level, asking them to break the word down into the relevant parts: graphemes, blends and diphthongs, and/or syllables.

● Haiku poems are another good way to focus on syllables. They must have no more than 17 syllables, and are arranged in patterns, most typically 5–7–5 syllables, such as this old Japanese haiku:

> *This snowy morning*
> *   that black crow I hate so much...*
> *But he's beautiful!*
>
> Matsuo Basho (1644–1694)

Word roots, prefixes and suffixes

Subject facts

So much for phonemes and graphemes. What humans are really about is meaning, and for meaning we need words. When looking at words for meaning, they are broken down into one or more 'morphemes'. A morpheme is the smallest unit of sound in any language that has 'semantic' significance; in other words, it has 'meaning'. In essence, it is enough to know that morphemes can be one of two things: root words (also called base words) and affixes. An affix is a unit of sound that has meaning, and comes in the form of prefixes or suffixes.

For example:

Happy is a single morpheme.
Unhappy has two morphemes, 'un-' and 'happy' – 'un-' is the prefix and 'happy' is the root.
Happily has two morphemes – 'happ(y)' (note the adjusted spelling in happily) and '-ly'. 'Happy' is the root word and '-ly' is a suffix.
Unhappily has three morphemes – 'un-', 'happ(y)' and '-ly'. 'Un-' is a prefix, 'happy' is the root word (with adjusted spelling), and '-ly' is the suffix.

Now, here's the interesting bit: 'un-', although not used on its own, does have meaning. The *OED* tells us that, as a prefix, 'un-' means *not*. Similarly, the suffix '-ly' denotes *the characteristic of*.

This is also where we can understand the role of other languages in forming our own, and why some people believe that learning Greek and Latin can help us to understand our own language so much the better. For example, 'hyper-' in Greek meaning *excessive*, gives us *hypersensitive*; or 'inter-' in Latin meaning between, gives us *international* and *intervention*.

As the following chart shows, these prefixes (there are roots and suffixes too) are interesting, but often lend themselves to more complex vocabulary.

Understanding words

Prefix	Origin	Meaning	Example
bio-	Greek	life	biology
micro-	Greek	small	microscope
pan-	Greek	all	panorama
therm-	Greek	heat	thermal
co-	Latin	together	coexist
dis-	Latin	not	disbelief
pre-	Latin	before	prepay
sub-	Latin	under	subway

There are many, many prefixes and suffixes. Some of the most common of each are listed below. As you look at them, try to think of other words that use them.

Common prefix	Meaning	Example
dis-	not, opposite	disappear
in-	into	inside
mis-	wrongly	mistake
non-	not	nonsense
pre-	before	preface
re-	again	reread
un-	not	undecided
up-	upwards	upturned

Common suffix	Meaning	Example
-able	can be done	reasonable
-ance	the act of	deliverance
-ful	full of	wonderful
-less	without	hopeless
-ly	the characteristic of	lovely
-ment	action or process	enjoyment
-ness	state or condition of	sadness
-ous	having the qualities of	joyous

Also, there are a few basic suffixes that we all use regularly:
- '-ed', to make the past tense for regular verbs,
  for example, *walked*
- '-er', to make a comparative for adjectives,
  for example, *smaller*
- '-est', to make a superlative for adjectives,
  for example, *smallest*
- '-ing', to make the present participle of verbs,
  for example, *walking*
- '-s' or '-es', for the plural form for nouns,
  for example, *books, watches*.

Generally, prefixes are 'derivational', meaning that they do not change the class of the word they are added to, such as *happy (adj)* becoming *unhappy (adj)*, whereas suffixes are usually 'inflectional', meaning that they **do** change the class of the word they are added to, such as *home (noun)* becoming *homeless (adj)*, or *enjoy (verb)* becoming *enjoyment (noun)*. The spelling rules for prefixes and suffixes are explained in Chapter 5.

Thinking about root words, suffixes and prefixes, we begin to see how we can use these morphemes to create larger vocabularies as we learn the meanings that they carry. Of course, it isn't that easy, this is English after all! You may have noticed that there are three different prefixes for *not* just in the small charts on page 62, used at different times for reasons that are sometimes logical, sometimes not.

Why you need to know these facts

● Understanding how words are built provides the foundation of a good vocabulary. Appreciating the small meanings and rules that govern how prefixes and suffixes combine with root words enables us to more readily decipher new words that we can then use effectively.

Vocabulary

Affix – a morpheme that is attached to a root word to form a new word.

Derivative – a word derived from another word.

Inflection – changes in the basic form of a word or the addition of an affix to reflect a grammatical feature.

Morpheme – a meaningful linguistic unit.

Prefix – morphemes attached to the beginning of root words.

Root word – the primary unit of a word, sometimes referred to as the base.

Semantic – having meaning in language.

Suffix – morphemes attached to the end of root words.

Amazing facts

Antidisestablishmentarianism is one of the longest words in the English dictionary, and has 28 letters, 12 syllables, and an impressive seven morphemes! Can you work out the meaning of each one?

Anti – dis – establish – ment – ari – an – ism

Common misconceptions

Remember that morphemes are not the same as syllables. Morphemes are units of meaning, syllables are units of pronunciation.

Handy tips

When breaking down words to help with spelling (see Chapter 6), be relaxed as to whether children break them down according to morphemes or syllables. Breaking down into morphemes is often more logical, but using syllables can feel more natural.

Teaching ideas

● Let the children become word detectives. Provide a list of multi-morpheme words and ask the children to break them down, using a suitable dictionary to find the root word and to identify the meaning of each morpheme.

● Create a language display, each week changing the focus morpheme (such as 'dis-', 'stop' or '-ful') and have children add words using the focus morpheme.

● Play games with cards bearing a range of prefixes, suffixes and root words. Can the children create real words? Can they spot false words, or indeed words that do not exist, but could have meaning. For example, *dislearn – to forget something you have learned(!)*

Word classes and families

Subject facts

Every word in English has its own class, depending on what it is being used for in a sentence. It is important for us to understand the different categories of words we might come across when referencing dictionaries, or indeed in trying to understand the relationships between words. Word classes are also referred to as 'parts of speech'.

Although grammar is not the focus of this book, we can use a simple sentence to illustrate all word classes.

The old man laughed heartily and walked towards me.

This sentence contains examples of all the main word classes. Definitions of these are given in the vocabulary section.

- *The* – determiner
- *old* – adjective
- *man* – noun
- *laughed* – verb
- *heartily* – adverb
- *and* – conjunction
- *towards* – preposition
- *me* – pronoun

The words in a word family are normally related to each other by a combination of form, grammar and meaning. Understanding them can help us build up spelling and vocabulary skills. Let's take a simple, three-letter, phonetic word like *run*.

Consulting the *OED* we immediately see that it is an irregular verb: *run, running, ran*, meaning to move at a speed faster than a walk. Next, we see that it has 12 further variations in meaning as a verb, such as *the bus runs every 15 minutes* and *that story will run in all tomorrow's newspapers*. Reading further, we see that it is also a noun with around a dozen meanings, such as *to go for a run* or *the rabbit lives in a run*, and so on. Moving on to phrases, there are many containing *run*, such as *to be run off one's feet* and *to run the gauntlet*. We then have many compound words: *run across, run into, run out, run-around* and *runaway* (note that some compounds words have spaces, some hyphens, and some are one word).

There are then new words derived from run: *runner* is a noun with multiple meanings; and *running* can also be a noun, an adjective, part of various compound words such as *running battle* and *running repairs*, as well as its verb form mentioned above. All in all, *run* and its family take up two whole pages of definitions in the *OED*.

Now let's look at a more complex word, the verb *to serve*. Sticking with the use of the word that means *to perform services or duties*, from this we get a broad family of words: *servant, server, servery, service, serviceable, servicewoman, serviceman, servitor, servitude* and *servomechanism*, not to mention several compound words, such as *service provider*. Not a bad list, and we can take it a bit further with prefixes, giving us *disservice, unserviceable*.

Why you need to know these facts

● As children move through primary school they will start to use increasingly complex grammatical sentences. Understanding the different classes of words can help them to consider both the correctness of their sentences, but also help them to source the appropriate rules to check their spellings. Also, understanding how word families work can become an effective route to help with spellings and quickly build up our vocabularies.

Vocabulary

Adjectives – describing words, such as *black* and *large*. They describe nouns.

Adverbs – describing words, such as *quickly* and *merrily*. They describe verbs.

Conjunctions – used to join phrases together, such as *but* and *for*.

Determiners – used to make nouns specific.

Nouns – naming words, such as *table* and *computer*. They identify objects.

Prepositions – indicate movement, time and place, such as *into*, *by* and *between*.

Pronouns – used in place of nouns, such as *she* and *it*.

Verbs – doing words, such as *throw* and *speak*. They identify actions.

Word family – a group of words related to each other by a combination of form, grammar and meaning.

Common misconceptions

Words that share spelling patterns, such as *back* and *crack*, are sometimes mistakenly referred to as belonging to the same word family. Remember that word families share combinations of form, grammar and meaning, not rhyming or spelling patterns.

Teaching ideas

There are many, many ideas for teaching about word classes. If you do not have resources at hand to help you, try asking children to identify word classes in any text at hand, including their own writing.

● Choose a suitable word and brainstorm what words might belong to its family. Then ask the children to analyse each word in the family and consider its class, its morphemes, whether it is compound or not (see opposite), and then investigate its origins. Encourage the children to check their own work using a suitable dictionary.

● Give the children a 'word of the day', for which they must write down as many related words for that family in a given time.

● Make sets of word cards for families of words. Distribute these randomly among the class, then ask the children to group themselves based on which word family they belong to.

Compound words

A compound word is created by bringing two existing words together, such as *policeman*, to create a new word that has its own meaning. It sounds easy, but as ever there are all sorts of variations and rules. A compound word can have a space in it (such as *compact disc*), a hyphen (such as *second-hand*), or just be one word (such as *earthquake*).

    Compound words take on various forms. Our knowledge of word classes will help our understanding of compound words, as will the role of the space, the hyphen and the apostrophe.

Word types	Examples
Noun-noun	fireman, newspaper, classroom
Noun-verb	breastfeeding, finger-painting
Verb-noun	breakfast, chewing gum
Verb-verb	can-do
Verb-adverb	fallout, readable
Verb-adjective	tumbledown, run ragged
Adverb-verb	intake, backtrack
Adjective-noun	fast food, second-hand, software, high chair
Adjective-verb	short-change

The apostrophe is used in a small number of cases when certain words are combined and in the process a sound is removed. This is known as 'elision'. We insert an apostrophe to denote the contraction where it replaces the missing letter or letters.

For example:

>   cannot – can't
>   is not – isn't
>   have not – haven't
>   would not – wouldn't
>   I am, you are, she is/he is, it is – I'm, you're, she's/he's, it's
>   we are, they are – we're, they're
>   we will – we'll
>   let us – let's

Three things to be aware of with apostrophes:

● *Will not* contracts to *won't*.

● Apostrophes are often put in the wrong place. Remember that they show where the letter has been removed. They do not show where the join has taken place: *wasn't* is correct; *was'nt* is incorrect.

● Be sure not to confuse apostrophe contractions with using the apostrophe to denote possession – for example, *That is Sally's car* (the car belongs to Sally). This use of the apostrophe is sometimes referred to as the *Saxon genitive*.

> ## Why you need to know these facts

● As with word families, spotting and building banks of compound words can quickly build up your spelling and vocabulary banks.

● Also, we tend to speak in contractions, so it is important to teach how they work so that children can clearly understand them in speech and casual writing.

Vocabulary

Compound word – a new word that is created by bringing two words together as one word, hyphenated or with a space between them.
Elision – the omission of a sound or syllable.
Saxon genitive – use of the apostrophe to show possession.

Common misconceptions

Words formed by combining parts of two words are not compound words, for example, *ginormous* comes from combining *gigantic* and *enormous*. These are called 'portmanteau' words, and often originate as slang.

Handy tips

Apostrophes are tricky to learn. Try to avoid lessons that try to show their different uses for contraction and possession – teach both cases separately. The best way to see if an apostrophe is used, and where, is to write what would be correct without one.

Teaching ideas

● Present the children with a range of compound words that they might find tricky, and ask them to split them into their separate parts and write down what meaning they think the compound word has, then check against a dictionary.

● Research the origins of compound words, including place names, and create a class display or book.

● Try finding or creating new compound words, especially relating to modern-day culture, such as double-click.

Special words

So far in this chapter we have seen how words are created and defined. English being the complex language it is, there are also a range of words that are somewhat special cases. In particular, we need to be very aware of words that are spelled and pronounced the same, but have different meanings; words that are spelled differently but sound the same; and words that share the same spelling but are pronounced differently.

● **Homonyms:** words that share the same spelling and pronunciation but have different meanings are called homonyms. Words such as *can*, *match*, *rock* and *watch* all have more than one meaning; they can belong to different word classes too.

● **Homophones:** words that have different spellings (as well as meanings) but sound the same: *aid/aide*, *by/bye*, *flour/flower* and *read/reed* are all homophones.

● **Homographs:** words that are spelled the same way but may be pronounced differently are called homographs, although there are not so many of these. Examples include ***lead*** *is a metal/****lead*** *me away*; ***close*** *the door/stand ****close*** *to it*.

The above cases are things to be aware of when we are spelling words. If it is vocabulary development and writing style we are considering, we need to be aware of 'antonyms' and 'synonyms'.

● **Antonyms:** words that are opposite in meaning, such as *big* and *little*.

● **Synonyms:** words that have similar meanings, such as *happy* and *joyful*. As covered in Chapter 3, a thesaurus is the ideal tool for referencing synonyms.

Why you need to know these facts

● Although tricky to remember, these groups and the common words that belong to them are worth learning as they are easy ones to trip up on when writing. When it comes to helping children improve their style, considering the ambiguity that using homonyms can create, as well as the power of synonyms, can help to improve the flow of their prose.

Vocabulary

Antonyms – words that have opposite meanings.
Homographs – words that have the same spelling but are pronounced differently.
Homonyms – words that have the same spelling but have different meanings.
Homophones – words that have different spellings but the same pronunciations.
Synonyms – words with identical or similar meanings.

Amazing facts

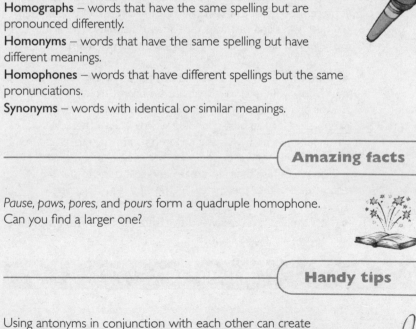

Pause, paws, pores, and *pours* form a quadruple homophone. Can you find a larger one?

Handy tips

Using antonyms in conjunction with each other can create powerful sentences. Look at the opening to Charles Dickens' *A Tale of Two Cities*:

> *It was the best of times, it was the worst of times, it was the age of wisdom, it was the age of foolishness, it was the epoch of belief, it was*

the epoch of incredulity, it was the season of Light, it was the season of Darkness, it was the spring of hope, it was the winter of despair, we had everything before us, we had nothing before us, we were all going direct to Heaven, we were all going direct the other way...

Teaching ideas

● It is not always advisable to teach homonyms, homophones and homographs explicitly – covering them together can often confuse children. Although the terms and their implications should be introduced at some time in the primary phase, it may be better to cover specific words in their usual contexts. The well-known example being *they're, there* and *their:* unless you are introducing a clear rule for how to remember which to use, you may find it more productive to cover the spelling of each one separately, although jokes and cartoons that draw on confused meanings can be helpful in drawing the children's attention to them.

● Synonyms are very much worth your attention. Most teachers are familiar with exercises that use synonyms to improve the power of a piece, but it can easily be overdone. Rather than simply plucking the best-sounding words from a thesaurus (or indeed memory), ask the children to improve texts according to the specific tone required, whether spooky, scary, gentle, and so on. Or ask them to create and edit texts to suit the character of either the writer or one of the protagonists.

● At a simpler level, use word cards to play synonym (or indeed antonym) pair games or snap.

Resources

The Cambridge Encyclopedia of the English Language by David Crystal (Cambridge University Press)
Spell It Out: The Singular Story of English Spelling by David Crystal (Profile Books)
Quick Fix for Phonics Wendy Jolliffe (Scholastic Ltd)
The Primary Teacher's Guide to Phonics Wendy Jolliffe (Scholastic Ltd)

The rules of spelling

We are now stepping into the rather delicate territory of spelling rules, which for many of us have been a source of persistent frustration since we first encountered them. The difficulties we have with English spelling boils down to two key aspects:

1. There are a lot of rules, and some of them are complex.
2. There are a significant number of words that break these rules.

These points can both be adequately exemplified by the nation's favourite spelling rule: *i before e except after c*, which works admirably for words like *belief* and *receive*, but regularly falls apart in words such as *efficient* and *height*.

In fact, there is a more complete version of this rule, and, as with many rules, we have to consider the pronunciation of the word in question. Expanding the above rule to say *if the sound is ee, use i before e except after c* helps a lot for all 'ie' and 'ei' words that make the sound /ee/. It is an improvement, though it still isn't much use for the words that don't make an /ee/ sound (and there are a few exceptions to the longer rule too). The net result (after all these years!) is that most people have given up on this rule, which is probably a good thing for teachers – it can't be easy to devise a motivating and useful lesson for it!

So, what rules *are* worth knowing? From a teacher's point of view, the more the better, although it is something of a linguistic minefield. From a child's point of view it is harder to say. Unless children are comfortable with the additional cognitive load that learning rules brings, there is certainly an argument for introducing them on a need-to-know basis. As ever, it will boil down to a combination of school policy, the child's aptitude, and teacher discretion.

The rules of spelling

Short and long vowels

Subject facts

There are approximately 15 different vowel sounds in English, ignoring dipthongs (see Chapter 4). Of these sounds there are short vowels and long vowels. The study of these can help enormously with understanding word construction.

● **Short-vowel sounds** – /a/, /e/,/i/, /o/, /u/ – are mainly made if they are in a closed syllable. That is, the syllable containing the vowel sound ends in one or more consonants. Examples of this are:

> bat, raft, den, legs, pill, sin, wind, con, plot, gut, trust

(Well done if you spotted the exception – *wind* can also be pronounced with a long-vowel /igh/ sound, as in *to wind up a clock*.) The 'closed syllable' rule gives rise to some other rules concerning consonants:
- 'f', 'l', 's' and 'z' are usually doubled at the end of short-vowel, one-syllable words, such as *tiff, pill, toss* and *buzz* (exceptions include *if, of, is* and *us*).
- For a short vowel in a one-syllable word, or the first syllable, ending in a /k/ sound, use 'ck', for example, *back, check, stick, flock, buck, backing, pecked, flicker, mocking, luckily*.
- The /j/ sound is spelt 'dge' if the word has one syllable, a short vowel, <u>and</u> there is no other consonant before the /j/. For example, *badge, ledge, ridge, lodge, fudge*. If not, the spelling for the /j/ sound is 'ge', for example, *large, merge*.

Unusual spellings for short-vowel sounds can be represented by two vowels together. Such as 'ea' together making the /e/ sound. For example, *head, bread, dead, health, stealth, wealth, feather, leather*. But, note that this is not always the case, for example, *reach, cheap*. The easiest approach here is to visualise the patterns.

Finally, and oddly, for historical reasons 'o' sometimes makes the /u/ sound, as in *love, done, come* and *money*.

● **Long-vowel sounds** are sometimes represented by graphemes 'a', 'e', 'i', 'o', 'u' when they are in open syllables. That is, a syllable that does not have a consonant at the end. Examples of this are:

able	*/a/ble/*
enough	*/e/nough/*
idol	*/i/dol/*
open	*/o/pen/*
universe	*/u/ni/verse/*

Long-vowel sounds are also made when the letter 'e' appears after a vowel-consonant combination, creating a split digraph. Contrast these pairs:

man/mane, pet/Pete, pin/pine, not/note, dud/dude

Note that the /e/ at the end remains silent, and it can also occur in multi-syllable words. For example:

amaze, concrete, polite, remote, dispute

There are several other ways of making the long-vowel sounds. The most common ways are shown below but beware, there are others (see page 57).

● The sound /ai/ can also be made with the letters 'ai' in the middle of words, and 'ay' at the end; such as *rain* and *straight*, and *day* and *play*.

● The sound /ee/ can also be made with the letters 'ee' and 'ea', but with little logic as to when and where, such as *meek* and *flee*, *teak* and *pea*.

● The sound /igh/ can also be made with the letter 'y', usually at the end of words such as *why, sky, clarify*; and also by 'igh', such as *high, fight, slight*.

● The sound /oa/ can also be made with the letters 'oe': *poem, toe*; 'oa': *soap, toast, floating*; or, often at the end of words, by 'ow': *tow, slow, follow*.

- The sound /oo/ isn't made very often, though the letters 'u' and 'e' are sometimes combined to form it at the end of words such as *value* and *argue*.

Why you need to know these facts

- There are around 20 vowel sounds in English, stemming from only five letters. As such, the phonetic rules attached to these letters form a strong foundation for all speaking and writing, and learning them can be beneficial for children's reading and writing.

Vocabulary

Long-vowel sounds – the vowel phonemes that have a greater duration when pronounced, such as /ay/ in *able*.
Short-vowel sounds – the vowel phonemes that have a shorter duration when pronounced, such as /a/ in *apple*.

Amazing facts

'The Great Vowel Shift' is the term used for the changes in pronunciation in English long vowels over the centuries of Middle English (see Chapter 1). In this period the way vowels were pronounced gradually changed, with some sounds becoming identical, giving rise to homophones such as *pane* and *pain*.

Common misconceptions

It is not always the case that two vowels together make a vowel digraph. If there are two distinct vowel sounds, for example, 'oi' as in *noise* it is called a diphthong (see Chapter 4).

Handy tips

Remember that all syllables have a vowel sound in them.

Teaching ideas

● Use rhyme to reinforce pronunciation of vowel sounds.

● Make a split digraph machine using strips of card with CVC words on and a template with spaces for the words and an 'e' after the spaces. Pull the strips through the machine, pronouncing the words before they go in, and then looking at the change when they are next to 'magic e'. Use this to reinforce the rule that with 'magic e' the vowel takes its name, without 'magic e' it makes its sound.

Consonants that make different sounds

Subject facts

We have already seen that vowels can make a range of sounds, depending on how the word is constructed, not to mention historical whimsy. The same variation occurs with most consonants, though some are more problematic than others. In particular, we are going to look at 'c' and 'g', both of which have different versions.

Contrast *cat* with *certain*, and *calendar* with *ceiling*. Or, looking at the middle of words, contrast *strict* with *efficient*, and *factory* with *fancy*.

We can see that 'c' makes an /s/ sound when it comes before 'i', 'e' or 'y', otherwise it represents a /k/ sound. This observation is often referred to as the 'c' rule and can also be applied to a word containing a double 'c'. For example, contrast *accident* with *accommodate*, or *accept* with *accumulate*.

Also, although words ending in 'e' normally drop the 'e' when adding a suffix that begins with a vowel, such as, *drive + able = drivable*, if there is a 'ce' ending, the 'e' has to stay in place to keep the 'c' sounding like 's', such as, *notice + able = noticeable*.

The letter 'g' presents similar variation based on the same rule. Contrast *goal* with *gist*, *grab* with *gentle*, or *granite* with *gymnasium*. Or, looking at the middle of words, compare *regret* with *regent*, *brag* with *age*, or *rags* with *enrage*.

But beware, there are lots of common 'g' words that break this rule, such as *get*, *give*, *girl*, and *forget* and *target* (both because of *get*).

Why you need to know these facts

● The letters 'c' and 'g' between them account for many spelling errors in children's writing, given their different roles in different words. By focusing just on these two letters you can introduce a range of rules and words that will immediately lift children's word-awareness and spelling abilities.

Common misconceptions

The /s/ sound at the end of words is hard to spell, as there are many 'se' words as 'ce' words, such as *cease*, *false*, *case*, contrasted with *prance*, *defence* or *ice*. This is one where the differences must simply be learned.

Handy tips

Remember, the difference between *practice/practise*, *advice/advise*, and *licence/license* is that the first in each pair shown here is a noun, the second a verb. To remember this, think that alphabetically **N** for noun comes before **V** for verb, just as **C** comes before **S**.

Teaching ideas

● A great way of remembering words that fall on one side of a rule or another is to have children make memorable sentences that contain as many of the words of that type as they possibly can, such as:

> In **such** *a* **false case** *it is* **nonsense** *to* **promise** *to* **cease** *the* **chase**.

Prefixes and suffixes

Subject facts

Prefixes and suffixes are explained in Chapter 4, and are generally not too problematic in spelling. One of the few easy spelling rules you'll ever come across is that prefixes do not affect spelling when added to the start of words. For example, *dis*allow; *re*pay; *un*assuming; *con*figure; *fore*arm. For the most part, adding prefixes does not usually change the word class, so a prefix added to a noun creates a new noun, and so on. The exception occurs when the lexical categories of the prefix and word are different, such as *en*slave, *a*blaze and *be*witch.

Suffixes can affect both the spelling of a word and class of the word, such as *true* (adj) + '-ly' = *truly* (adv). The good news, however, is that most of the rules for adding suffixes are consistent. There are exceptions, of course, but the following rules are worth knowing.

● Short-vowel, one-syllable words have their last letter doubled when adding a vowel suffix:

> *hot + -er = hotter*   *big + -est = biggest*
>
> *get + -ing = getting*

The rules of spelling

But not when adding a consonant suffix:

    good + -ness = goodness   *hope + -ful = hopeful*

● For words ending in 'l' with one vowel before the 'l', then double the 'l' when adding a vowel suffix:

    travel + -er = traveller   *marvel + -ous = marvellous*

But if there are two vowels before the 'l' do not double it:

    steal + -ing = stealing   *feel + -ing = feeling*

● Split digraphs drop the 'e' when adding a vowel suffix, but not a consonant suffix.

    care + -ing = caring   *care + -less = careless*

● For words ending in 'y' if there is a consonant before the 'y' change the 'y' to an 'i' when adding prefixes.

    lovely + -est = loveliest   *ugly + -er = uglier*

    merry + -ment = merriment

Contrast these changes with:

    obey + -ed = obeyed   *pay + -ment = payment*

    boy + -ish = boyish

There is an exception to the rule, of course. When adding '-ing' do not change the 'y' even if it is preceded by a consonant. Look at the word *try*:

    try + -ed = tried   *try + -ing = trying*

And, there are some words that break the rule altogether, most notably:

    pay + -ed = paid   *day + -ly = daily*

● Letters are sometimes doubled when adding suffixes. We have already seen that 'l' is sometimes doubled depending on the base word, but a more tricky rule applies to some two-syllable words. When we pronounce a word, the stress falls on one syllable. The stress in these words is in bold:

*mou**tain**, for**get**, **ord**er, com**mit***

For two-syllable words, if the stress falls on the second syllable and the suffix begins with a vowel, double the last letter. For example, *forget* + *-ing* = *forgetting* but *forget* + *-ful* = *forgetful*, and *commit* + *-ed* = *committed* but *commit* + *-ment* = *commitment*; whereas *mountain* + *-ous* = *mountainous* and *order* + *-ing* = *ordering*.

Beyond these rules, the spelling of the base word is not changed by adding a suffix, such as, *treat* + *-ment* = *treatment*; *still* + *-ness* = *stillness*; *result* + *-ing* = *resulting*, and so on, though you should be aware of irregularities and one-offs, noting them as you come across them.

Why you need to know these facts

● As children's language skills grow they will need to construct words to facilitate the more complex meanings that they wish to communicate. They will do this initially through speaking and, as we know, rules and spelling conventions are not learned alongside the newly acquired vocabulary. By introducing rules governing prefixes and suffixes systematically, we can support children in ensuring that in their writing they are able to convey the breadth and depth of their thoughts.

Amazing facts

The consideration of where stress falls can affect spelling, but it is critical for spoken language to be clear and effective. For example, the word *present* with the first syllable stressed means a gift, but with the second syllable stressed means to offer something. Try this: say **pre**sent and pre**sent**.

The rules of spelling

Vocabulary

Stress – the syllable that receives emphasis when speaking, such as *obey*.

Handy tips

Rather than teaching the rule about stressing syllables to primary-aged children, you may find it easier simply to look at words together and decide which is right/wrong (for example, corrected/correctted). However, with the relevant word lists in front of the class, you could use this as an opportunity to discuss stress and emphasis with older children.

Teaching ideas

● Short-vowel, one-syllable words double the last letter. Tie this rule in to teaching about comparative and superlative adjectives, such as *fat, fatter, fattest.*

● Supply lists of words with the same prefix and ask the children to write them in alphabetical order.

● Give the children a piece of text with the prefixes mixed up – ask them to highlight (and correct) the mistakes.

Plurals

Subject facts

Forming plurals introduces another small set of rules. Everyone knows that to make a plural we must add an /s/ sound, for example, *dog* + -s = *dogs, computer* + -s = *computers,* and so on.

- Nouns which end in an 's' sound, however, require '-es' to form a plural. For example, *bus* + *-s* = *buses*. Most importantly, we should note that the 'es' rule also applies to /ch/, /sh/, /k/s/ and /z/. For example, *lunch* + *-s* = *lunches*; *bush* + *-s* = *bushes*; *fox* + *-s* = *foxes*; *quiz* + *-s* = *quizzes*. You may have noticed, also, that in adding '-es' we also add a syllable to the word.

- Words ending in 'y' have their own small set of rules. If the letter preceding the 'y' is a vowel, to make a plural just add an '-s'. For example, *day* + *-s* = *days*; *boy* + *-s* = *boys*; *survey* + *-s* = *surveys*. However, if the letter preceding the 'y' is a consonant, we must drop the 'y' and add '-ies', for example, *city* + *-s* = *cities*; *cherry* + *-s* = *cherries*.

- Words ending in 'o' have '-es' added to them when plural, such as *echoes, tomatoes, potatoes, volcanoes*. However, if there is another vowel before the final 'o' (*radio*), or the word is abbreviated (*disco*), or the word is a musical instrument (*piano*), just add '-s', such as *radios, discos, pianos*.

- Notable oddities for plurals include a small range of words ending in the /f/ sound that change to '-ves', such as *half* + *-s* = *halves*, *life* + *-s* = *lives* and *knife* + *-s* = *knives*. Many words ending in 'f' just take add '-s', such as *belief* + *-s* = *beliefs*, and *roof* + *-s* = *roofs*. And oddly, some words can take either spelling, such as *hoofs* or *hooves* and *dwarf* or *dwarves*.
  Some common words give us irregular plurals, such as *children, women, teeth* and *feet*. Also, there are some words which don't change for the plural form, such as *sheep, news, grass,* and *scissors*.

Why you need to know these facts

As mentioned in Chapter 2, children establish rules for constructing words, and they may simplify plurals at first. Unfortunately, the simple rule for adding '-s' has many exceptions and variations. None are that difficult (they are relatively straightforward), but we do need to teach these to ensure that children's language is lucid and clear as they develop their speech and writing.

The rules of spelling

Handy tips

Remember that when adding an apostrophe to denote possession to a plural ending in 's', there is no need for another 's'. For example, *There are two boys' hats.* Contrast this with an irregular plural: *There are two children's hats.*

Teaching ideas

● Make cards with '-s' and '-es' on them, along with themed sets of noun cards for the children to put together.

● Create a plurals display, showing the different types previously listed. Each morning, list a number of words on the whiteboard, and ask the children to consider the correct plural form for each. Once ready, discuss each in turn, adding large written versions of each onto the display.

● Ask the children to practise writing simple sentences that pluralise objects, noting any grammatical changes that might accompany them. For example, *The girl was eating a baked potato* becomes *The girls were eating baked potatoes.*

Silent letters

Subject facts

Finally, we need to consider silent letters, which must be such a curse for those trying to learn English as a second or foreign language, let alone children for whom it is a first language. Amazingly, most letters of the alphabet appear silently in some or other words and these grapheme representations are often taught as alternatives in phonics, such as 'mb' for /m/.

Silent letters tend to fall into several categories, the first being simply odd – they don't even look right, such as silent 'k' at the start of some words, and silent 'b' at the end, for example, *knight, knee, comb* and *numb*. Double letters too, in effect, contain one silent letter.

There are a small number of silent letters that are useful in distinguishing word meanings, for example, *bee/be, damn/dam, tinny/tiny*. And, of course, there is the use of the letter 'e' at the end of a word which changes short vowels to long vowels, such as *pin/pine*.

Why you need to know these facts

- Silent letters will cause readers and writers problems. Often there is no option but to learn them as the oddities they are. It is up to teachers to judge how explicitly to draw children's attention to them.

Vocabulary

Silent letters – letters which make no sound in a particular word.

Amazing facts

Most silent letters are there due to their historical origins, when they would most likely have been pronounced.

The rules of spelling

Handy tip

For children who are having difficulties with silent letters, set up a page in their notebooks for silent-letter words (usually having encountered them in error, reading or writing). As they write down these words, encourage the children to sound out the silent letters as a memory-aid for spelling. For example, *an-swer, is-land*.

Teaching ideas

● Play silent letter bingo by giving each child a word grid, with some of them containing silent letters.

● Silent letters cause problems with reading as much as writing. Be vigilant in finding them in texts as well as children's writing, and create a class dictionary of silent letters, where children can add their own tips for how they have memorised them.

Resources

Getting to Grips with Spelling by Catherine Hilton and Margaret Hyder (Letts).
Aimed at adults, this is a handy book for understanding the basics and improving your own spelling.
The Cambridge Encyclopaedia of the English Language by David Crystal (Cambridge University Press)
Spell it Yourself by GT Hawker (Chambers)
The Primary Teacher's Guide to Grammar and Punctuation by Sebastien Melia (Scholastic Ltd)

Teaching spelling

In devising and monitoring a whole-school spelling programme, schools do not just want it to be effective, they also need it to be efficient. As the previous chapter indicated, spelling is a complex business, and there are only so many hours in the school day. Given that there are lots of more interesting things competing for the children's attention and memory demands, how can their spelling skills be developed, while keeping them engaged and motivated? (Or, indeed, avoiding negative attitudes to writing.)

Furthermore, most teachers find that they need to provide differentiated spelling programmes for children, from ability groups down to individual, personalised programmes. For this to be effective, educators need to understand the broad stages of language development, as well as being discerning in their planning, and knowledgeable in selecting the best resources to support their work.

Stages of spelling development

Subject facts

Various models have been developed to suggest the typical stages of spelling development, and it is relatively easy to consider these alongside children's oral and reading developments. Children's spelling development is, of course, entirely contingent on their exposure to language and text, and indeed the opportunity to play with and practise writing. With these opportunities presumed, a rough progression in spelling skills is given overleaf. Note that not everyone uses these terms, although they are common:

Pre-communicative

Between three and five-plus years, most children start to show awareness of words and their role in communication. In their play they make a range of marks that gradually show an understanding of what text is; make a distinction between drawing and spelling; show an awareness of the directionality of writing; and for some, demonstrate a growing range of letters that they can reproduce. Typically, this stage does not represent an awareness of how different graphemes make particular sounds.

Semi-phonetic

From around four to six-plus years, children typically develop an understanding of the alphabet and letter formation. They demonstrate a growing comprehension of letter/sound representation by spelling simple words in ways that show some understanding of the main sounds in those words.

Phonetic

tis   si   mY   GRANY

HoS   aND   iTis   Si   MoNTNT

tY   RT   SLEB   aND

IT,   IS   dRK   aNd

mY   GRANY   Hom   iS
NÍs

As the name suggests, from five-plus years, children start to write phonetically, using most of the alphabet in their writing. They start writing simple words correctly, using lower and upper-case letters in unusual ways to convey their ideas. (Teachers at this stage often become very adept at reading passages full of unusual spellings!)

Transitional

A pricess in the Army
A few years ago there was a pricess who Wanted
to Joun the Army But her perants Woud not
let her. She had an elda brother Who said
you cant Joun the army yore a girle. you
male shovanest pig She said. At last there
perants gave up. all right they said you
can Joun the army The next day
She pased her bags and Went to Joun the
army. The Rejamant She Jouned Was the paris.

Between the ages of six and eleven years old, children typically display increased competence in writing common words correctly. They show an increasing grasp of a wide range of structures and letter patterns, using them effectively in their writing. Although inconsistencies and errors still regularly occur, children in this phase show an increasing ability to use visual and semantic clues to support their spelling.

Correct

> Its a hot day and weve Just had a probelom.
>
> It's been sorted out now But I will tell you
> It all Started yesterday when paul, Susan, and sheridan
> had Just come back from the mill.
> we went into the girls bedroom and then into the frontroom.
> we heard a noise from upstairs, paul said it's a ghost and
> laythed, But then a man came down the stairs

At around ten years or later, children can show proficiency in their everyday writing, employing a wide range of strategies for self-correcting their work, aided by competent proofreading and dictionary skills. Although tricky words and new, more complex vocabulary can still present difficulties, uncommon letter patterns and irregularities are overcome using their visual memory skills.

It is important to note the skills that effective spellers have, relevant to their age-range:

- good auditory discrimination
- good visual memory
- an understanding of letter patterns
- the ability to divide words into syllables
- an understanding of word construction and modification
- an awareness of, and ability to, construct meaning.

Why you need to know these facts

- As a classroom teacher you have to bring two things together: the children in front of you, with their range of aptitudes and experiences, and the curriculum you are required to deliver. First and foremost, you must be aware of each child's abilities and needs in order to plan appropriate, differentiated materials.

● The stages of spelling development outlined previously are written very much with UK education systems in mind, and comparing children against these criteria can be a useful first step in assessing their needs. Ways and means of doing this are presented in the next section of this chapter.

Vocabulary

Pre-communicative – the early stage of spelling, where young children show awareness of letters.

Semi-phonetic – an increasing but inconsistent awareness of the alphabet in children's writing.

Phonetic – the stage of spelling using direct grapheme/phoneme representation.

Transitional – children's progression to more complex spelling skills.

Correct – the stage at which children are competent spellers, including strategies for self-correction.

Semantic – having meaning in language.

Handy tip

Never underestimate the value of speaking in supporting spelling. Pronunciation often contains the clues, as well as aiding the effective memorisation of words.

Teaching ideas

Obviously, teachers will use a wide range of activities as part of their literacy teaching. As such, the following broad suggestions are structured around the stages outlined in the previous section:

● **Pre-communicative:** allow children plenty of opportunities to be involved in role-play activities that involve texts, such as going to the doctors (prescriptions) and going to cafes (menus), or in sending birthday cards and other notes. It isn't important what marks they make on the paper, more that the concept of text is integral to their play.

● **Semi-phonetic:** continue with the approach outlined in the Pre-communicative stage, and encourage children to write about things that interest them, ideally observing them while they 'write', and talking about their work. Combine this with structured phonemic awareness activities to develop knowledge of grampheme-phoneme correspondences.

● **Phonetic:** introduce small writing tasks based on children's lives and recent experiences in the classroom, using the opportunity to show and discuss correct spellings for simpler words. Begin to focus on good handwriting practice.

● **Transitional:** encourage this stage of development by asking children to write more for each other, displaying their work and making class books. Continue to develop good handwriting skills, and use poetry to focus on different letter patterns which rhyme.

● **Correct:** classroom practice at this stage should focus on routines and expectations that promote independence and self-awareness, encouraging children to critically reflect on their spellings (alongside the structure and meaning of their texts) and to self-correct using their favoured strategies.

Planning for spelling

Subject facts

A debate worth having in all primary schools is this: *should we explicitly teach children the rules of spelling, and if so at what ages should these rules be introduced?*

Whether you gave an instinctive *yes, no* or *maybe* to the question, consider this: the above prompt uses the word *explicitly* as opposed to *implicitly.* In other words, should you be actually presenting the myriad of rules to your class and where and why to use them, along with the terminology involved, or should you simply be guiding the children through the language, in much the same way as we learn to speak without being explicitly taught grammar.

If you believe in the explicit approach, you will need to ensure your school has a thorough, high-quality scheme of work in place that is being followed consistently from year to year. If you believe in the implicit approach – in other words, covering all the key aspects of spelling without clearly presenting the actual rules themselves – you will need to be sure that the children have the necessary strategies to help themselves when they run into uncertainty. Either way, most teachers agree that the primary ingredient is as much exposure to language as possible, and most schools probably fall somewhere in between the two extremes, with a structured programme of word lists being used through the school, often with the children having their 10-a-week to practise, with key rules being presented as appropriate.

What elements might we find in a whole-school policy and/or scheme of work for spelling?

Firstly, the school's philosophy and approach to teaching spelling should be clearly identified, with consistent classroom practices outlined appropriate to each age range. This should include:

- Links with (or indeed be part of) the school's policies for literacy, teaching and learning, special educational needs and marking.
- Explicit identification of how children are to be taught spelling, whether via specific lessons, integration with other literacy lessons or subjects, structured word lists, or via children's own work.
- The school's preferred (and obligatory) methods and schedules for the assessment of spelling.
- The school's approach for setting and monitoring personal targets for children.
- Procedures, approaches and resources for addressing specific difficulties in spelling.
- Also, the school's position on which resources (home-grown or commercial) can be used, and why, should be evident. This should include any software or hardware owned by the school, specifically aimed at spelling improvement.
- Guidance on marking work and feedback to children should be clear. Does the school expect teachers to provide written feedback on all work, or should work

be reviewed alongside children and oral feedback given? Where spelling is concerned, how should teachers go about identifying spelling errors, and how should children respond, and how many spelling errors should teachers point out? (There can be nothing worse for a child who is thinking and writing, using language that is new to them, to have it returned to them splattered in marks and corrections.)

- Finally, the role of parents/carers should be identified. Most schools will issue information and possibly homework based around practising spellings. Schools have little control over how homework is done and other prevailing attitudes to school in the home, which although generally positive is not consistent. As such, it is very important that spelling work delegated to homework is done so with care.

Moving on to the long and medium-term plans that teachers will use for any one year group, elements that may refer to spelling will include term-by-term and week-by-week plans for spelling lessons, resources, word lists, and subject/topic related vocabulary, with daily plans providing specific detail as appropriate. Depending on the overall philosophy and approach of the school, in daily classroom life spelling will be addressed in one or more of the following forms:

- specific sessions focused on common letter patterns, word families, spelling rules and useful techniques.
- regular (usually daily) brief sessions focused on specific words or letter patterns.
- addressing spellings within the context of children's written work.
- focused spelling practice and tests.
- acquiring new word forms through reading.

Day-by-day, most teachers will then plan differentiated spelling work according to their baseline and ongoing child assessments. For many reasons this will usually involve grouping children in one way or another, according to spelling age, specific difficulties, and attitudes or aptitudes.

In reality, most schools use a mixture of the above, varying their approach according to age ranges and abilities. The critical factors for success being effective planning, teacher competence, child readiness and resource quality.

Why you need to know these facts

● Different countries often have quite radically differing approaches to education. This can oscillate from the extreme of nationally prescribed resources, timetables and methodologies, to minimal state intervention. In the UK, the prevailing approach is of moderate governmental guidance, a reasonable degree of autonomy for teachers, and fairly high levels of accountability. The implication of this for schools is that they must, through their own efforts or via consultation and collaboration, develop effective and informed approaches to teaching and learning. In preparing schemes of work and lessons for spelling, just like any other area of learning, they must be able to seek advice when needed, write effective policies, and critically reflect on their work.

Handy tips

Avoid reinventing the wheel! Seek help from colleagues, advisors and online forums when devising schemes of work and policies. Even better, if you know of schools with great practice already in place, talk to them.

Evaluating and using spelling resources

Subject facts

If you were to lock yourself away for a weekend and immerse yourself in the catalogues and websites of UK educational publishers, the type of spelling resources you are likely to encounter fall into several categories:
- complete schemes of work for literacy, addressing reading, writing and spelling, including a wide range of resources
- complete schemes of work for spelling
- small series of books providing supplementary spelling skills/practice

- one-off books tackling specific aspects of spelling
- tactile resources, such as blocks, tiles and interactive charts
- software aimed at providing in-depth hierarchies of spelling lists and monitoring child performance. Some such software will even attempt to diagnose weaknesses and suggest next steps
- software for practising spelling via interactive games.

With a school's philosophy and approach to learning clearly established and a clear spelling policy in place, resources will be needed to fulfil these aims. Schools often use a mish-mash of purchased and home-made resources; usually to good effect. However, in the hustle and bustle of daily school life, it can be difficult to reflect critically on the effectiveness of these resources. Ideally, teachers should apply intense scrutiny to resources before buying them in the first place, though given that most schools will already be using a range of resources, evaluating the existing ones is a good starting point.

Broadly speaking, commercial educational resources are either core or supplementary. Core resources aim to provide a complete solution to a particular area of learning; usually involve a fairly wide range of resources (often making them substantial and expensive); and may sometimes need specific teacher guidance or training to utilise them effectively. Supplementary resources are usually smaller and cheaper, and typically focus on quite specific areas of the curriculum, such as games to practise CVC words, or tricky words for older children.

The advantage of using a core resource for a scheme of work, spelling or otherwise, is that it allows you to be consistent and comprehensive of subject coverage, and once familiarity has developed, it can free-up teacher time for other tasks. The disadvantage is that core resources can be too prescriptive and restricting, and can be difficult to extend or replace should curriculum demands change.

Supplementary resources are useful for adding variety and interest, and giving you new routes into specific areas of learning. They are usually more adaptable too, making them more accessible to different teachers. Conversely, they can be fragmentary unless they are used in conjunction with a secure scheme of work.

Here is a useful checklist for evaluating existing or new educational resources. Most teachers automatically whizz through this list without noticing every time they pick up an educational resource, but it is worth using it for thoroughness, especially when purchasing expensive schemes of work.

- Does the resource fit in with our statutory obligations?
- Does its pedagogic approach concur with our own attitudes to teaching and learning?
- Does it fit in with areas of our current practice that we plan to maintain?
- Will it bring anything extra to our usual teaching practice?
- Is it pitched appropriately for the intended age group(s) and ability ranges in our school?
- Is it well-presented, thorough, interesting and structured in a way that is appropriate to our needs?
- Is it adaptable? In other words, is it easy to modify or is it rigid and prescriptive (and does this matter)?
- Does it facilitate appropriate differentiation?
- Does it support assessment?
- What are its weaknesses? (All resources have these, so identifying them and deciding whether they are acceptable to you is essential.)

Key aspects to check in spelling resources

While the above checklist works for any educational resource, in considering spelling resources, core or supplementary, it is critical to be confident that some or all of the following criteria are covered:

- Does it focus on teaching words appropriate to the children's current levels of performance?
- Does it explicitly teach spelling patterns?
- Is it arranged in small, manageable chunks?
- Does it provide plenty of opportunity for practice and feedback?
- Does it recap previously learned words?
- Does it help the children to apply and generalise newly acquired spelling skills?
- Does it include dictionary skills?
- Will it sustain the children's interest and motivation?

Why you need to know these facts

● If you carried out a survey of what makes a good teacher, what might be recognised?

Subject knowledge	✓
Understanding child development.	✓
A broad range of secure pedagogic techniques	✓
An ability to manage a large workload and keep smiling (and a thousand other skills)	✓
The ability to conceive and create effective educational resources	?

Hands up anyone who has spent evenings and weekends making worksheets, flashcards, PowerPoint presentations and other resources for use in the classroom? All teachers have done it at some time or another, and it's admirable, but crazy. There are enough good educational resources out there to fulfil the majority of your needs. Indeed, many staffrooms and school resource bases are full of such resources; it is knowing how to evaluate and implement them effectively that matters.

Vocabulary

Core resources – provide a comprehensive solution to a curriculum subject.
Supplementary resources – provide specific reinforcement, support or extension for aspects of a subject.

Common misconceptions

Here's an old cliché that gets banded around now and then:

A good teacher can make an interesting lesson using nothing more than a paper bag.

I don't think so! No doubt a good teacher can engage children and introduce some interesting phenomena and ideas using minimal resources, but for sustained, effective engagement of a class of 30 children over the six years of primary school, you need rich, engaging resources.

Useful strategies

Subject facts

As we develop into proficient writers we will not have a clear mental inventory of every word we can and cannot spell correctly. We could devote a lot of classroom time to learning every letter pattern and every spelling rule, and while there is no doubt that understanding these is important, they don't stick for everyone. As such, a range of methods have evolved which different people draw on from time to time to help with their spelling. Learning spellings has three broad aspects – auditory, visual and semantics (meaning) – and different methods work for different words (and indeed for different people). These are broadly outlined on the following pages, giving you a range of ideas to help consolidate children's knowledge and understanding.

Sound it out (auditory and visual)
Particularly with younger children, this should be standard practice (see Chapter 2), using grapheme-phoneme correspondence to support spelling.

Show the shapes (visual)

By drawing shapes around words you can help children to recognise letter shapes within words, and how they affect the overall word.

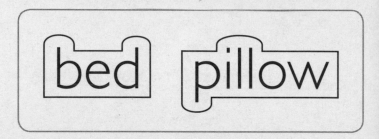

Use rhyme and analogy (auditory and visual)

Again, especially with infants in mind, this is a great technique for reinforcing sounds and letter patterns via rhyming words.

Syllabification (auditory and visual)

As mentioned in previous chapters, syllables are the units that we tend to break words into when speaking. They do not necessarily correspond to a word's letter patterns or morphemes (units of meaning). Syllabification is breaking words down into their syllables to help with spelling them.

As a quick guide, remember that all syllables have a vowel sound in them (including that made by 'y'). There are a range of rules for dividing up syllables, and many are covered in Chapter 5, but people tend to develop their own ways to help them divide words. Look at this range of words with their suggested syllabifications:

Example	Syllables
pen	pen
pencil	pen / cil
penalty	pen / al / ty
penetrating	pen / e / tra / ting
penitentiary	pen / i / ten / tiar / y

Notice that vowels can form a syllable on their own.

Whether learning new words or recalling them, encourage children to write them down and pronounce each syllable. This makes longer words more manageable, focuses attention on the sounds and encourages greater analysis of word structures.

You can take this approach a stage further by having children write each syllable in a different colour, or writing the different syllables on cards and joining them together.

Exaggerated pronunciation (auditory and visual)

When children find specific words difficult, in particular where the phonic rules seem complex, pronouncing the words in an exaggerated way (usually in syllables) can help. In fact, as adults this is often what we do when someone we know asks us for a spelling, such as *des/crip/tion*, *ma/chi/ne* and *int/er/est/ing*.

Create word families (visual)

Although word families are defined as sharing a common root word, children might also benefit from creating families for words that share letter patterns or rhyme.

Analyse it (morphology)

For any one spelling, write down the root word, the morphemes and the homophones.

Consider meaning (morphology)

Particularly for homonyms, encourage children to consider them in context, such as *I had a **pain** in my side*, contrasted with *the ball broke a **pane** of glass*.

Check it yourself (visual)

We need to instil children with independence and self-awareness, not to mention honing their visual memory. As we become competent readers and spellers we know instinctively if a word looks right or wrong. For example, the sentence below is legible even though only have half of each word is visible.

If you can read this sentence it proves the point

Mnemonics

A mnemonic is something that assists our memory. There are people who can remember the order of a whole pack of cards, and they often do this by creating a story around the cards as they turn them over. It is the story that helps with the memorising. There is a small range of mnemonic techniques listed below that you might draw on from time to time to help children remember trickier spellings.

● **Funny sayings:** Creating sayings or sentences that emphasise a spelling pattern can help with all of those words, such as:

Please **add** your **add**ress.
Do you bel**ie**ve a l**ie**?
A**cc**o**mm**odate accommodates two **C**s and two **M**s.
Knights **kn**it **kn**ickers!
Use your **ear**s to h**ear**.

This technique can also be used for distinguishing between words that present different problems, such as:

You should go to the lib**rar**y in Feb**rua**ry.
Please pro**cee**d to the next pro**ce**dure.

● **Acronyms:** An acronym is a word made from the initial letters of a group of words; a phrase or sentence, usually presented in upper case, such as BBC. Occasionally, we see these used for spelling tricky words. For example:

BECAUSE:	RHYTHM:
Big	Rhythm
Elephants	Helps
Can	Your
Always	Two
Understand	Hips
Small	Move
Elephants	

Some people find creating their own acronyms is useful, if there are words they persistently struggle with.

● **Chanting:** People often find that chanting a word to themselves can help with spelling, especially if the words have a good rhythm to them. Try it with these words: *ba-na-na*; *mi-ni-mum*; *M-i-ss-i-ss-i-pp-i*.

● **Handwriting:** Good handwriting skills with correct letter formation is generally considered an excellent aide to improved spelling skills. Be sure to insist that any spelling practice includes correct letter formation and joining, whatever age the children are.

Why you need to know these facts

● If taught in dull, repetitive ways spelling can break the spirit of even the most optimistic of children. Employing a range of approaches, activities and mnemonics, all delivered in short bursts, can keep children motivated.

Vocabulary

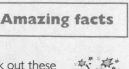

Acronym – a real or new word made by combining the initial letters of a phrase.
Mnemonic – a technique for jogging the memory.
Syllabification – breaking down words into syllables.

Amazing facts

Dyslexia doesn't have to be a barrier to success. Check out these famous dyslexics: Richard Branson (entrepreneur); Noel Gallagher (musician); Keira Knightley (actress); Richard Rogers (architect).

Handy tips

We have the potential to have extraordinary memories, and good spelling is mainly about memory. As such, it is worth considering how well memory can be developed per se. The artist Maggi Hambling said that she was able to draw people from memory so well because she'd practised it so much when she was a student – going to the pub and carefully watching people, then returning to her studio and trying to draw and paint them from memory. It is very hard to know if techniques focused purely on memory improvement can work in the classroom, but exercises related to this are usually interesting to children, such as looking at a picture for one minute then describing it to someone.

Teaching ideas

● **LASACASAWAC!** If you use the age-old 'Look Cover Write Check' approach, change it to **L**ook **A**nd **S**ay **A**nd **C**over **A**nd **S**ay **A**nd **W**rite **A**nd **C**heck. Remember, the auditory aspect of spelling is essential.

● If you issue regular word lists to your class, try varying the way in which they must practise these. Here are a few suggestions:
  • Dice Game: Throw the dice; write your next word in that style.
    1. Best joined-up writing
    2. Bubble writing
    3. Capitals
    4. Syllables (or base word) in different colours
    5. How many phonemes (or syllables)?
    6. Fancy writing
  • Write a simple sentence for each word. (You could have all your word list written on individual cards – pick out two or three words and include them in one sentence.)
  • Put your words in alphabetical order. (Order your word cards and/or write them out.)
  • Find the words in a wordsearch, or create your own using

your word list (there are lots of free wordsearch makers on the internet).

- Play Pelmanism. Write all the words on separate cards, two for each word. Place them face down and mix them up. Take it in turns to turn two cards over and read the words. When you find a matching pair spell the word to keep the cards.
- Type your words on the computer, writing each in a different colour/font/size.
- Write banks of root words, prefixes and suffixes on cards. Ask children to find those that can go together to make new words and write them down, adjusting spellings as necessary.

Assessing spelling

Subject facts

Some people find spelling more difficult than others. As outlined in previous chapters this is for several reasons:
- English is a difficult and irregular language some of the time
- people have a variation in childhood experiences, affecting the quality of their early development and awareness of language
- our brains are all different
- some people struggle to overcome gaps and inconsistencies in their knowledge and understanding of English as they grow older
- we pick up habits and misunderstandings that are often hard to shake off.

As such, the primary teacher's job is a complicated one. To teach effectively we need to identify what the children already know and their current level of ability, and to do this we need to assess them accurately. In assessing spelling, teachers use both formal and informal approaches: spelling tests and the children's own writing. Both approaches have their merits and weaknesses. Without wishing to dwell too much on the obvious, first and foremost teachers need to be aware of the purpose of an assessment. In current-day primary schools assessments are not just for the child's benefit. They are also performed to measure the effectiveness of teaching, resources, and the school itself. (They are even used to measure the country, but that is a slightly different matter!)

Assessments can use qualitative or quantitative information. Qualitative assessments tend to be based on professional judgements and anecdotes gathered from a range of sources, whereas quantitative, as the word suggests, are based on scores and grades.

Assessments can be formative – to help us understand a child's abilities and/or difficulties and consider what they need next, or summative – to help us measure a child's current abilities.

A third type of assessment is diagnostic. These tests are typically made where there are concerns about children having specific difficulties, such as dyslexia, with a view to implementing focused interventions if necessary.

Formative assessments

Meaningful formative assessment typically involves teacher (and child) judgement and opinion, and usually leads to child-focused feedback. It can involve carefully marking work and adding appropriate comments, or it can be ad hoc face-to-face guidance. Meaningful, correctly pitched feedback can be critical to effective progression for children, as can self-awareness of their current achievement and attainment. As such, the success of formative assessment lies in the quality of the language used in giving feedback to children. Contrast *you are Level 3 in literacy* with *you are using some great language in describing atmosphere, but we need to recap on how to use commas correctly as well as the rules for adding '-ly' to make adverbs* – a bit exaggerated, but the drift is obvious.

Summative assessments

By contrast, summative assessments are usually grade-related, often entering the realms of standardised tests along with their computer printouts and statistical charts. This is not to denigrate summative testing, but to acknowledge that its standardised nature makes it a rather impersonal instrument. Standardised assessments are typically used to provide a baseline assessment and to monitor progress. Typically, they provide a spelling age, a standardised score, and a percentile score for any child who completes them.

Spelling ages are an easy way of conveying a child's performance relative to national averages, although experience has shown them to be misleading at the top of the range, and they are limited in accurately ranking performance.

Standardised scores are useful in allowing schools to monitor performance against other tests. They allow different sets of data to be compared, and are usually quite complex to calculate or use pre-configured charts. The value-added rankings of schools' league tables use standardised scores, typically with 100 as the average.

Percentile scores, as the name suggests, positions children on a scale of 1–100. These scores can then be plotted on a bell-curve distribution, which is considered to be a typical representation of the range of all cases. So, for example, on the chart below, dividing all cases into eight equal divisions, 34.13% of cases (for us, children) are positioned in the third one-eighth of the curve. We can see from the curve that very low and very high scores are less frequent than those around the average of 50%.

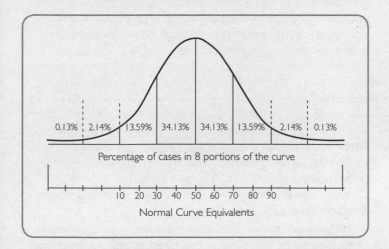

Percentage of cases in 8 portions of the curve

Normal Curve Equivalents

Diagnostic assessments

Diagnostic assessments are usually used when teachers and parents/carers have specific concerns about an aspect of a child's work or behaviour. In spelling, diagnostic assessments will look at which kind of words are being misspelled and what sort of mistakes are being made. Where more fundamental concerns are raised regarding children's linguistic abilities, initial diagnostic assessments focus on children's abilities to respond to rhythm, alliteration, syllables, and phonemic manipulation.

The next section covers a range of typical spelling errors and problems, and suggests approaches for each.

Why you need to know these facts

- Teachers assess their children all the time, constantly picking up on their moods, errors and successes. The end of year report requires considerable skill to generalise this myriad of details into a few succinct paragraphs. In daily classroom life teachers are regularly giving children verbal or written formative feedback to guide them to their next steps; alongside these judgements standardised assessments can be useful in providing a more objective view of how children are progressing. For this process to be effective teachers need to understand the needs and implications of different assessments. Furthermore, where more pronounced special educational needs are evident, meetings with SENCOs and other specialists will involve discussing the procedure and outcomes of such assessment.

Vocabulary

Baseline assessment – a summative assessment aimed at establishing the ability ranges in a child or cohort, usually performed at the start of an academic year.

Diagnostic assessment – a specialised assessment to identify specific difficulties.

Formative assessment – carried out with the primary objective of deciding which next steps of teaching and learning are needed.

Percentile score – a 'ranking' from 1–100 which usually provides a bell-curve distribution of scores when those for many children are combined.

Spelling age – an easy-to-understand guide to show whether children are performing above, below or at their 'expected' ability.

Standardised score – as with spelling age, but with 100 as the average. These are used for statistical interpretation of large amounts of data from many children.

Summative assessment – carried out with the primary objective of establishing baselines and monitoring children's progress, and (sometimes) the performance of teachers and schools.

Amazing facts

Half of the population are below average! No matter how much we improve education, and no matter how much our collective intelligence improves, that statement will always be true. (And, of course, half the population are above average too…)

Common misconceptions

It is easy to muddle the type and purpose of assessments. This is mainly because we tend to make formative judgements using any information we have, including that from summative assessments. In an area such as spelling this is not really a problem (in fact, it could save you time) – the main thing is to aim to be as precise as possible as to the nature of each child's current knowledge and abilities. However, we must be very mindful not to jump to conclusions from limited amounts of information.

Handy tips

Don't let the children get hung up on spelling. It sounds obvious, but people who are aware of their shortcomings in spelling can curb their own writing, failing to demonstrate the scope of their vocabulary and their linguistic abilities.

Identifying and supporting difficulties, encouraging independence

Subject facts

As we have seen from preceding chapters, classroom teachers will encounter children with a wide range of difficulties with their spellings and, as outlined previously, good assessments can support teachers in developing accurate individual profiles and an understanding of any specific difficulties.

In considering children's errors, it is important to be clear whether any mistakes are typical for the age range, one-off errors, or if a child is consistently making the same type of errors. Obviously, most children will have vocabularies that are beyond their spelling capabilities and we do not want to quash their enthusiasm to draw on their word banks. As such, teachers must be careful in their decisions as to which spelling mistakes to focus on. If a six-year-old child wrote the word *freekwentli* it would probably be enough to be impressed that the child is using such a word. Pointing out the correct, complex spelling would not necessarily be beneficial at that stage.

General spelling errors made by most children at some stage can be classified:

Errors	Examples of misspellings	Suggested actions
Letter reversal (most typically 'b' and 'd')	*deb* for *bed*	Put flicks at the start of letters to raise awareness of letter formation. Use picture card prompts.
Phonetic spelling	*walkt sed nutrishun*	Review rules and letter patterns as appropriate, or ignore if vocabulary is ambitious for the age range.

Errors	Examples of misspellings	Suggested actions
Confusion over blends, silent letter and double letters	*wen niting acomodation*	Review phonetic guidelines and silent letter rules. Introduce techniques for remembering tricky words.
Misuse of a rule	*goed beautyful hopefuly*	Review rules or irregular words if appropriate to the age range.
Misuse of an exception	*truely flowwing sieze*	Review exception and introduce appropriate strategy.
Unfamiliarity with irregular words	*becaws Febury*	Review and introduce appropriate strategy.
Confusion of homonyms	*It is **there** car. He **road** on a little **hoarse**.*	Review homonyms and their alternatives in correct contexts.
Misuse of punctuation	*is'nt house's fire-man*	Review rules of using punctuation, showing words without contractions where appropriate.

Specific learning difficulties may give rise to more complex spelling problems. You may find that there is no clear solution to helping children with specific and/or significant problems, though certain types of error can be helped with specific interventions. Ultimately though, it is a case of knowing the child and considering what works best.

Given the levels of frustration that can ensue for those who find writing tricky or laborious, provide as much general support as you can:

- provide spelling aids where appropriate
- provide word banks specific to children's needs, their stage of development, and the task in hand
- for longer pieces of writing allow them to dictate, and scribe for them at times – it is important that they can

still express themselves, and having a scribe can help some children greatly.

Specific errors	Suggested actions
Difficulties in remembering or reproducing letters	Intensive work to develop knowledge of the alphabet; use physical actions to trace letters; rhymes about letter construction; associated words for individual letter sounds; and letter tiles to form simple words.
Difficulties with writing legibly	Work on fine-motor skills, including continued handwriting practice. Consider the suitability of pen/pencil – helpful add-on grips are available, as well as left-handed pens and pencils.
Jumbled letter order	Use visual approaches and reinforce phonetic rules as much as possible.
Problems with hearing particular sounds	As well as hearing tests this may require intensive action, encouraging children to watch the mouth of the speaker when focusing on specific words in spelling sessions.
Non-phonetic or erratic spelling	Use visual and auditory approaches to work on phonetic pronunciation of blends and patterns.
Inconsistent spelling of the same words	Target key high-frequency words that need to be learned as 'whole' words.

With all of the above issues, teachers must choose how much they need to intervene, and how much they should encourage independent correction by children. This requires judgement on a case-by-case basis, although it is advisable to encourage relative degrees of independence as children progress through primary school. There are many strands to achieving independence in spelling, and we have already discussed using word charts, dictionaries, thesauruses and technology, as well as a range of strategies and techniques to support children in acquiring and using new words (such as, listening and reading, and speaking and writing). All of these become very powerful if we can instil in children an understanding of how to review their own work, giving them proofreading and checking strategies that encourage them to identify and correct their own spellings (see Teaching ideas).

For children to work towards using any strategy or tool independently, teachers need to carefully structure their introduction to it. This simple checklist can be useful

- the purpose of the strategy needs to be explained. Remember, don't be afraid to use the metalanguage
- tool or strategy use should be clearly modelled, with the teacher 'thinking aloud' through each strategy step
- children should be allowed plenty of practice in small, regular chunks
- observe children as they use the strategy, providing relevant feedback as needed
- monitor and assess strategy use.

Why you need to know these facts

● Although we are able to use a range of strategies and resources to support children's spelling skills, ultimately we want to encourage independent learning as much as possible as children progress through primary school. To be clear, this is not to say that the role or skills of teachers become less important as children move through school, but greater child resilience and resourcefulness are now considered essential skills for daily life, and equipping children with such skills can allow future teachers to focus on subject content more dynamically and engagingly.

Vocabulary

Metalanguage – the technical language used to explain a subject.

Handy tips

When marking children's writing it is important to consider how many spelling mistakes you should point out. For a child with difficulties, receiving feedback full of underlined or corrected errors is likely to be more demoralising than constructive. Try to focus on a limited number of mistakes that would be most beneficial for them to correct.

Teaching ideas

● Organise a system that, on a regular basis, allows children to list three words that they have recently misspelled, and have an allocated slot, perhaps during afternoon register, when they can practise their three-a-day. When they are confident with these spellings they should move on to focus on correcting new errors.

● Create clearly available word charts focusing on age-appropriate high-frequency words, tricky words or topic focused words.

● Introduce children to a range of proofreading techniques so that they might choose the one that suits them best, such as using a sheet of card with a thin window cut in it to exclude the rest of the text, or (less dramatically) 'scrolling' down the page with a ruler to allow a clearer focus on each line, or reading the text backwards to stop the brain 'auto-correcting'.

● Introduce a strategy for children to proofread their own work that involves a small range of different marks to indicate errors, such as, a circle for an error they are certain of and a wiggly underline for words that they are unsure about. Taking this further, to really get the children thinking, have them indicate their errors with different symbols according to the type of error – phonological, morphological or meaning.

Resources

Understanding Spelling by Olivia O'Sullivan and Anne Thomas (Routledge)

Scholastic Literacy Skills: Handwriting series by Amanda McLeod, et al. (Scholastic Ltd)

The Word Wasp: For Teachers and Parents by Harry Cowling (H J Cowling). Aimed at anyone aged eight-plus with language difficulties, including dyslexia. This is a passionate (self-published) book with a very well-structured, phonetic based approach to teaching the rules and structures of spelling.

Developing strong vocabularies

Most teachers would agree that strong linguistic capabilities are probably the most important attributes for children to learn in order to develop their knowledge and understanding across the school curriculum. Even in subjects involving creativity or logic, the ability to discuss and explain our thinking effectively can be very beneficial (this is not to say that art or music always needs to be explained). Unfortunately, children arrive at school with differing language skills and vocabularies, and their teachers must create classroom environments and deliver lessons that support and challenge everyone. This requires children to develop a range of fundamental skills:

- the ability to listen attentively
- the confidence, or at very least security, to be able to speak freely and openly when appropriate
- strategies for deciphering new words
- legible, flowing handwriting
- effective memory skills.

With structures in place to develop the above skills, schools must provide stimulating, language-rich environments which allow children to encounter and reproduce a widely varied vocabulary in a range of engaging contexts.

Focusing on words

Subject facts

Children of all ages can benefit from explicitly focusing on words and their meanings. Focusing specifically on vocabulary can involve the following activity types:

- practising and playing with the sounds and rhythms of words
- singing songs
- playing word memory games
- researching and sorting words according to their origins, families, classes and spelling
- dissecting words: looking at roots, prefixes and suffixes
- looking at word associations such as synonyms and antonyms,
- effective use of dictionaries, thesauruses and technology
- using crosswords, wordsearches, language games and word lists
- completing cloze texts: either with or without word banks
- looking at text types and considering vocabulary choices.

A word of caution: one-off activities focusing on word types are fine, but ideally should be part of a much larger range of activities where language is used for meaningful purposes.

Why you need to know these facts

- Varying the stimulation and activities around any subject is usually a good thing, and vocabulary acquisition is no different. Having a back-up supply of one-off activities will keep children on their toes and potentially engender a love of words.

Common misconceptions

Don't confuse vocabulary and spelling. It's better to know and use a word you can't spell than not.

Handy tips

If you have a 'word of the day', make them tricky and/or unusual. Keep them in a bank that builds up over the school year, and award house points, or whatever your system of reward, for unprompted use of any words from the bank.

- There are a huge number of vocabulary focused games. Try to choose games relevant to the age range, and also ones that focus on aural and written forms.
  - I-spy with a twist – *I spy something that rhymes with…* – for example, *chair/hair.*
  - Nouns vs verbs – one person has to name a noun, the next has to state a relevant verb. For example, *spoon – eat; dog – bark.*
  - String it out – how long can you describe an object without naming it before someone guesses it? For example, *This is a large animal that you wouldn't see very often in this country. It eats leaves, and high trees don't bother it. It is grey…*
  - Shopping list – start off by saying, *I went shopping and bought a…* The next person must repeat this and add a new item. How many items can you add to the list before one person forgets? This game can be played with variations, such as new words following alphabetical order, or words for a specific topic only.
  - Play Pelmanism with cue cards containing all the target vocabulary for a new topic.
  - Use index cards to create a class dictionary that children can add new words to as they encounter them, including meanings. Each week, review all the new words added. Use the opportunity to consider synonyms and antonyms, and consider how the new words might be used in context.

Speaking and listening

Although the focus of this chapter is vocabulary, it is important not to think that it is something to be addressed in isolation. Yes, there are focused activities and techniques that we can use to try and develop children's word stores, but we must always remember that to comprehend and communicate effectively requires an understanding of words, which can be used alongside the rules of grammar to create meaning. It is in receiving, and then using, these words in context that gives them purpose and links language to thinking.

Speaking

Speaking is possibly the most undervalued skill of all. Talking, alongside thinking, helps us to interact with the world and to consolidate our understanding of facts and phenomena. Voices are tricky to manage in the classroom, where quiet is sometimes regarded as a plus. However, talking is much faster than writing, and, when well-facilitated, can allow children to access different levels of vocabulary, both subject-related and communicative.

- **Explaining work:** Either talking about how we have produced something, or otherwise, can be very useful. Alternatively, a powerful aide to learning can be talking through a task while doing it. This can really focus the mind and consolidate understanding.

- **Delivering presentations:** Individually or in a group, this is good for both building confidence and language skills.

- **Storytelling:** This should not be purely the domain of the teacher. It is relatively easy to introduce children to the basic skills of storytelling, and to build these skills through structured sessions.

- **Reciting poems:** Either well-known ones or children's own, is also a useful way of exercising memory and vocabulary.

- **Singing and chanting:** Particularly effective for young children to develop a sense of rhythm and rhyme, generally and in relation to language.

Listening

In order to gain new words or knowledge we use our eyes and ears. For effective learning, these need effective input, and schools can provide this in various ways.

- **Teacher talk:** Provides opportunities for introducing, modelling and reinforcing new vocabulary. We should not be afraid to use language that will be tricky for children, whatever the area of learning being covered, the job of the teacher is to use language that is rich and engaging. Remember – children are capable of absorbing many new words per day, and hearing teachers talk using appropriate vocabulary in meaningful contexts will support this learning.

- **Peer talk:** In work and play children will listen to each other, although as we all know, some are much better at this than others. Appropriate classroom routines and well-modelled language from teachers will help children to develop their listening skills and word acquisition.

- **Recorded materials:** These are often under-used in schools. Most of us are familiar with using recorded stories and videos as part of the learning environment from time to time, but how many schools have large banks of audiobooks in their library for children to take home? Just as children like reading stories, they like listening to them too, and not just when they are young. And what is more, just as children will sometimes watch the same DVD a number of times, they will listen to a favourite story or book many times over. Try talking to a child who has done this; it is likely that they will be able to tell you the whole plot with ease, and they will use vocabulary and expressions from the story.

Oral interaction

The generic speaking and listening activities listed above do not necessarily involve the sort of interaction where speaking and listening are taking place at once. In particular, debate and drama both involve considerable interaction.

- **Discussing and debating:** These often sit in the mind as something for grown-ups, but it need not be so. Well-structured debates based around (say) philosophical ideas, historical events or environmental concerns can be highly stimulating for children. The trick for the primary teacher is choosing a meaningful and engaging topic and structuring the debate to involve everyone, with rules that help maintain focus.

● **Drama:** This is used to fantastic effect in many schools. Remember that drama activities can be short – they don't have to be lengthy plays. Working from pre-written play scripts can be great for vocabulary development, as can having children create their own dramatic vignettes based on cue cards for specific scenes or character traits.

For all of the above areas, it is possible to provide effective support to ensure that children's work is developmental. Teachers are generally comfortable in scaffolding children's writing using templates and frames, but it can be trickier for speaking and listening. Ideally, aspects of the school's literacy policy will provide a degree of guidance on effective classroom practice for such activities, such as 'rules' for listening, effective scene setting and teacher modelling, methods for ensuring participation, access to relevant word banks and cues for prompts. Implemented well and thoroughly, this can lead to efficient and effective progress in speaking and listening skills – and effective use of growing vocabularies – as children move through primary school.

Why you need to know these facts

● The tendency towards spelling and vocabulary development is often through word lists. These have their place and can work up to a point, but to acquire active vocabularies we need to use language. Structuring a range of speaking and listening experiences for children around interactive, dynamic use of language will not only engage children more, it will help to enhance new vocabulary and its use.

Common misconceptions

Observing many maths lessons, you'd be forgiven for believing that many teachers feel that talking doesn't greatly benefit learning in maths. This is partially due to the often abstract curriculum attached to maths, as well as the structure of many resources. In fact, talk can be very productive in maths: children can collaborate on purposeful maths-oriented tasks, such as furnishing and costing a bedroom to budget, explain their workings, and discuss strategies using the appropriate vocabulary.

Handy tips

Keep it snappy. Hands up those who have had to sit through an assembly that goes on and on – we all know how it feels. OK, it doesn't happen most of the time, but ensuring that teacher utterances are meaningful, focused and interesting will obviously help to sustain children's attention and learning.

Teaching ideas

● Develop an audiobook borrowing section in your school library.

● Allow children opportunities to 'write orally'. To do so, you will need to scribe for them, or they can record their own stories for playback to peers.

● For older children, structuring classroom debates as if in a courtroom is a great way in to discussing historical dilemmas: assign different roles to different children, including jury and media. For example, was Howard Carter right to open the tomb of Tutankhamen?

● To encourage actively identifying good vocabulary, create a wall display (or if you're feeling brave an interactive website) of children's favourite quotes from books.

Reading

Subject facts

There are a wide range of text types that are encountered in schools, and each has their own nuances of vocabulary and style. Newspapers tend to use Standard English (see Chapter 8), whereas fiction may incorporate slang and dialect. Letters, reports and non-fiction all have their own stylistic quirks and unique vocabularies, as well as the variation that each writer brings to them. Poetry is often concerned with metre and cadence – the structure, rhythm and sounds made by words. Gradually introducing children to all of these text types as they move through primary school will both stimulate and broaden their vocabularies. Teachers need to be critical and informed when choosing and rejecting texts for classroom use.

When reading we are more likely to come across specific words that we may not understand or know how to pronounce. In the early years of primary, teaching reading effectively and thoroughly will make a significant difference to the rest of children's entire education. As children progress to a wider range of texts, it is essential to equip them with phonic and contextual decoding skills, as they should be regularly encountering new and difficult words throughout their time at primary (and indeed secondary) school. In everyday reading for work and pleasure it is impossible to control the vocabulary that children will encounter, and approaches for dealing with new words need to be taught. Teaching the routines isn't difficult, but instilling the discipline to use them can be. Try having an agreed and well-known set of 'rules' for what children should do when they encounter a new word. Use some or all of these, depending on age range:

What to do if you find an unfamiliar word:
- *Make sure you can pronounce it correctly. Look at the letter patterns. Can you sound it out?*
- *Read the sentence it is in. Can you guess its meaning?*
- *Use a dictionary, looking carefully to find the right meaning. Does it make sense to you?*
- *Does it look like any other words you know?*

- *What sort of word is it?*
- *Are there any other words that mean the same thing?*

If you are comfortable with such procedures, you can extend them by having each child create their own bank of new words, including definitions, and encourage them to reuse them in their own writing.

Understanding words in context is a skill taught from a fairly early age. As children progress through primary school they need to appreciate that 'context' may mean several sentences before and after the word they do not understand. Look at this example.

He was a rather capricious man.

Being a definitive statement, we have no clues to the meaning of the word *capricious*. Let's review the sentence before this:

Brian could be an infuriating friend. He was a rather capricious man.

We now have some clues, but they are not enough to deduce the correct meaning of *capricious*. Let's look at the sentence after this too:

Brian could be an infuriating friend. He was a rather capricious man. He had been one for changing his mind ever since David had known him.

We might not be able to discover the precise meaning of the word, but we can reasonably deduce that *capricious* means to be changeable. In fact, it means to be prone to sudden and unaccountable changes of mood or behaviour.

The different skills of reading (for example, scanning) are not the focus of this book, but it is worth noting the benefits of reading aloud towards vocabulary development. It requires us to focus on every word, intoning it correctly for the context and written style, using inflection for dramatic effect and personal interpretation. Try to provide children with ample opportunity to read aloud. They might read their work to each other or the class, read poems while others enact them, or read excerpts from fiction or non-fiction.

Why you need to know these facts

- As children grow into independent readers, we have less and less control over what words they will encounter, and it may often be easier for them to bypass a word rather than understand it. Missing a word or two out from the overall text often won't inhibit their enjoyment or understanding of it. Teaching good habits and techniques (as well as a love of discovering new words) can help equip children with the tools they need to understand new words on their own.

Vocabulary

Cadence – the rhythm and tone of poetry.
Inflection – changing the pitch and tone of the voice, usually for expressive purposes.
Metre – the structure and beats of a poem.

Handy tips

Set up word logs for children, maybe in the back of their spelling or handwriting books if your school has these. Here they can note new words they encounter in their reading, adding meanings and any synonyms.

Teaching ideas

- When reading, discussing and reviewing fiction encourage the children think about the author's style – how do they achieve what they do, and how does their choice of vocabulary help?

- Stage small plays or dramatic vignettes. Reading from pre-written playscripts is a great way to develop confidence and technique in reading with tone and emphasis.

- Using suitable poems, have children work in groups to read (or recite) them with dramatic inflection.

Writing

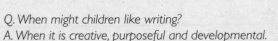

Subject facts

Most children like to read. By contrast, many children do not enjoy writing. Why might this be the case? At school, and beyond, writing is sometimes used for a different purpose than in daily life: in school it is used to show what we know and what has been covered. Our success in history, for example, may be affected by our ability to write well. Tests and exams may be here to stay, but with technology replacing blackboards and chalk, it is no longer necessary to have a class of 30 children all copying the same thing as written by the teacher (or answering the same set of questions from a textbook). This approach may have benefits now and then, but we will be doing children a favour whenever we move away from writing as a tedious task to being a purposeful action.

Q. When might children like writing?
A. When it is creative, purposeful and developmental.

This is not to say that we should be cosseting children from self-discipline and hard work, but we should be creating motivating situations for them to write in. Interesting topics do this, drama does this (very well), and good poetry and stories inspire it too. Furthermore, the physical acts of writing and typing are usually slower than speaking, and although this might allow us to be more measured in our communications, it does not always mean that children are able to fully express themselves.

From the point of view of vocabulary development, there are several things you can do to support children when they write with one or more of the following:
- provide high-quality stimulation
- provide model texts
- scaffold the task with suitable writing frames
- provide vocabulary banks relevant to the topic
- provide banks of 'wow' words: more imaginative vocabulary

that can enhance their work.

Considering the initial stimulation for writing for a purpose, contrast these two approaches to a piece of writing about the sinking of the *Mary Rose*. Both have their strengths and weaknesses depending on your views and desired outcomes.

> *Two Year 4 classes go to visit the Mary Rose in Portsmouth. They spend an enjoyable day looking around, making notes about the artefacts and listening to information about the ship and its history.*
>
> *Back at school, one class uses their notes to write an account of their trip, structured into different sections such as what the salvaged goods tell us about daily life in Tudor times, why the ship sank, and so on.*
>
> *The other class, back at school, enacts the sinking in a drama session, each child with pre-assigned roles, such as observers on the shore, King Henry and his aides, or survivors of the wreck. Afterwards they write diaries and letters telling of their ordeal, supported with writing templates and vocabulary banks.*

Both of the above approaches have strengths and weaknesses. From the point of view of language development, in particular vocabulary, consider which might be more effective in your context.

Finally, help your children to learn how to review and edit their own writing with vocabulary in mind. Identify words that could be improved to clarify meaning or to make their texts more engaging, and consider conciseness: writing with brevity and accuracy, reducing jargon and avoiding verbosity.

Why you need to know these facts

● Ensuring that children see writing as something useful, engaging and powerful, requires carefully planned tasks and effective resources. Without structured support and established improvement routines many children's writing can use simple and uninteresting vocabulary, and will not truly reflect their abilities or show any development of personal styles.

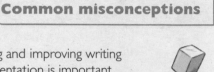

Vocabulary

Jargon – the technical language used by a particular set of people or an organisation.
Verbosity – the tendency to use too many words.

Common misconceptions

Presentation isn't everything. Revisiting and improving writing should be done selectively. While presentation is important, not all work has to be done in 'best'. If children are to review and improve a piece, they need to be well-versed in how to do so, using their word banks and thesauruses to good effect.

Handy tips

Avoid writing for the sake of it. That might sound like a statement of the obvious, but excessive time spent on writing tasks that are not engaging or purposeful, or indeed rewriting in 'neat', can create a very negative perception in children. 'What I did in the holidays' might be a reasonable icebreaker at the start of a new year, but it also comes with an implicit message of tediousness.

Teaching ideas

- When marking writing, try to mark with vocabulary development in mind. Pick out two or three good words per written piece, or identify one or two places where the child could have used better language. Supporting specific difficulties with vocabulary acquisition is likely to require specialist interventions (see Chapter 2).

- Rather than having children write whole stories, focus just on beginnings, endings, scenes or characters, creating small, accessible class books of children's work.

● Give older children texts that need improvement. They need to develop this skill for their own work, and using third-party texts can be a more secure starting point. Extend this activity from altering specific words to rewriting whole sentences using Standard English or figurative language where appropriate.

Resources

Getting to Grips with Vocabulary by Catherine Hilton and Margaret Hyder (Letts). Aimed at adults, this is a useful book of ideas and advice for improving your own vocabulary.
Did I Hear you Write by Michael Rosen (Andre Deutsch)
The Meaning Makers by Gordon Wells (Hodder and Stoughton)
Developing Writing 3–13 by Roger Beard (Hodder and Stoughton)
Looking into Language by Bain, Fitzgerald & Taylor (Hodder and Stoughton)
The Primary Teacher's Guide to Understanding Texts by Huw Thomas (Scholastic Ltd)
The Primary Teacher's Guide to Speaking and Listening by Roger McDonald (Scholastic Ltd)
The Primary Teacher's Guide to Writing by Eileen Jones (Scholastic Ltd)

Vocabulary in context

If it wasn't enough to have a language of over half a million words to get to grips with, we have also evolved several ways of using it. Often without realising it, we encounter and use English in different forms throughout the school day – the 'correct' English of the morning news, the banter of the staffroom, formal meetings with outside agencies, and so on. These forms of English simultaneously provide us with substantial teaching challenges and opportunities, and help us set children squarely on the road to fluency and independence.

Figurative language

Subject facts

By figurative language we mean language that goes beyond its literal meaning, such as *a square meal*, which is nonsense if taken literally. How much to use such language is a tricky dilemma for teachers. By and large, it isn't considered standard English, but it is ever present in daily life. For infant teachers, in particular, teaching *about* figurative language can be tricky. But looking at it and understanding it can be great fun. It can liven up drama no end, cause plenty of laughter, and, of course, it enriches our understanding of our language.

An idiom is a figure of speech that has a non-literal meaning, such as, *we were on tenterhooks*. Taken literally this means nothing, but we use it to suggest being in a state of tension and uncertainty, while awaiting an outcome. Where such figurative language forms a complete expression, such as, *the early bird gets the worm,* it is called a saying or a proverb, used to illustrate a truth or common occurrence. When an idiom or proverb is overused and starts to lose its power it becomes a cliché (watch some interviews after a sporting or talent contest and you'll probably hear a few of these).

Specific lessons focused on these features of language may be hard, but it is possible to weave them into topic work, as their origins are usually historical. For example, there are a large number of expressions that originate with seafaring people (the term *square meal* actually comes from the square plates that were used on tables with edges to stop the plates falling off when the boat rocked); from work (*tenterhooks* refers to hooks and frames known as *tenters* that were used to stretch wool while it was drying); and the law, for example, *by hook or by crook* referred to means by which the poor were allowed to collect dead wood from the forest floor.

Other types of figurative language include metaphors, which use words outside of their intended meaning for effect, such as, *a blanket of snow, a heart of stone* or *frozen with fear*. These are easily confused with similes, which use *like* or *as* to suggest comparison: *like a whirlwind* or *as old as the hills*. Also worth knowing about is personification: using human attributes and actions to enliven language, such as, *the dawn crept over the hill*, and onomatopoeia, in which words sound like what they are trying to convey, such as *crunch, meow* or *hiss*. All of these techniques can be used to good effect in descriptive writing.

Why you need to know these facts

- As children progress through primary school, the development of their figurative language can make their communications more interesting, varied and powerful. It is also no bad thing for them to raise their awareness of how their language came to be the way it is, and to appreciate that such language can be used to good effect.

Vocabulary

Cliché – an overused idiom or expression.

Idiom – an expression that is not meant literally.

Metaphor – non-literal use of language to help describe something, such as *he was stony faced*.

Onomatopoeia – when words sound like what they stand for, such as, *bark*.

Personification – to give human attributes to something being described.

Proverb – an idiomatic saying that is complete in its own right.

Simile – a non-literal comparison using *like* or *as*, such as, *ears like radars* or *as hard as nails*.

Amazing facts

How about this for the world's longest cliché, by master-linguist David Crystal? How many clichés can you spot? Have you ever used any of these?

If I may venture an opinion, when all is said and done, it would ill become me to suggest that I should come down like a ton of bricks, as large as life and twice as natural, and make a mountain out of a molehill on the issue. From time immemorial, in point of fact, the object of the exercise, as sure as eggs are eggs, has been, first and foremost, to take the bull by the horns and spell it out loud and clear. At the end of the day, the point of the exercise is to tell it like it is, lay it on the line, put it on the table – putting it in a nutshell, drop a bombshell and get down to the nitty-gritty, the bottom line. I think I can honestly say, without fear or favour, that I have left no stone unturned, kept my nose firmly to the grindstone, and stuck to my last, lock stock and barrel, hook line and sinker. This is not to beat about the bush or upset the apple cart, but to give the green light to the calm before the storm, to hit the nail on the head, to bite the bullet, and thus at the drop of a hat to snatch victory from the jaws of defeat.

That's it. Take it or leave it. On your own head be it. All good things must come to an end. I must love you and leave you. I kid you not. Don't call us, we'll call you. And I don't mean maybe. Am I right, or am I right?

Common misconceptions

Shakespeare is full of clichés. This wasn't true at the time, in fact, many clichés that are used today, for example, *neither a borrower nor a lender be*, were created by Shakespeare. It is the use and abuse of subsequent generations that has gradually devalued his words.

Teaching ideas

● Encourage children to be idiom detectives. Guess at, then research the meanings of idioms, and illustrate the accepted meaning alongside the historic and/or literal meaning (this can be fun). Build up a class book.

● Challenge children to write a letter home as a pirate on a galleon. How many seafaring phrases can they use in their literal sense? (Have the phrases on display.)

● Display lists of metaphors and similes and model to children how they can make their language more vivid by incorporating them. Encourage the children to create their own metaphors and similes.

● Create a list of onomatopoeic words, and write a scene or a poem about a haunted house. Look at how the sounds create atmosphere.

● Spot the cliché. Set scenarios for children to rehearse a mock interview after certain sporting or talent show achievements. Who can use the most clichés? Can the children spot each one?

Subject-specific language

Subject facts

For each curriculum area in each year group of the primary school, well-defined vocabularies are needed. It is fine to display this vocabulary in the classroom, but more importantly you need to use it. Teachers need to model the good use of subject language and children need to reproduce it in their work. Science and the humanities, in particular, have a wide range of specialist vocabulary and terminology, as well as using certain common words more frequently than in everyday discourse.

By providing information and brainstorming early in any unit of work you can create word and phrase banks that will be useful in subsequent discussion and writing.

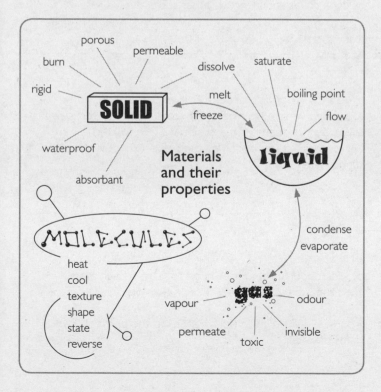

Why you need to know these facts

- For children to access any curriculum area, they need to know its language. By explicitly presenting the language associated with any topic or curriculum area, you will both support children's learning and extend their vocabularies.

Common misconceptions

Spelling doesn't always come first. This is not so much a misconception as a consideration of focus. It isn't as important for children to be able to spell *multiplication, condensation* or *chronology*, as to know what the words imply and to be able to use them in context. In other words, don't let spelling difficulties hinder a child's confidence in other subjects.

Handy tips

Have a display or flipchart at the front of the class, with vocabulary written on separate sheets for each subject being covered at the moment. If appropriate, give some children the responsibility for displaying the correct sheet for the appropriate lesson.

Teaching ideas

By linking strong literacy activities to other subjects, you can provide opportunities for children to learn facts in more interesting and meaningful ways. For example:

- Create a video guide (for an alien) to the different physical states of water.

• Write a leaflet about the approaching Vikings; warning people about their ways.

• Write a poetic description of the development of a river speeded up into five minutes.

• In art, describe a Van Gogh painting using only similes.

Formal English

Subject facts

We must ensure that children can distinguish between different styles of writing, and understand why styles are used. Formal English is used when a serious tone is needed, when we don't know the person we are addressing (including writing for a general audience), and for giving precise instructions. As such, the tone of formal language is usually neutral and precise. Politicians and lawyers use formal English as part of their daily work, in debates, speeches and questioning, though this can also slip in to *legalese* – jargon-filled English.

Children will be aware of some of the nuances of formal language from watching news programmes, reading instructions and so on. Tasks that support them in speaking and writing in these ways can help make their understanding more explicit. Just as for other curriculum subjects (see Chapter 7), providing word banks for formal English will help; as will practice in writing concisely, such as newspaper articles and letter writing. For speaking and listening, develop tasks that include simulated interviews, telephone calls appropriate to children's ages and abilities. Try to provide a wide range of texts written in formal English, picking out the key vocabulary that creates tone, and develop opportunities for children to edit and 'formalise' their own texts.

Why you need to know these facts

- In daily life we effortlessly switch our attention between formal and everyday English, but when we are forced to complete tasks that require formal English, we can discover it is harder than we might have thought. Explicitly teaching about the nuances of formal English can support children as they move towards independence in English.

Vocabulary

Formal English – a tone and style of language required for formal situations.
Legalese – language full of terminology pertaining to the subject.

Amazing facts

RP – received pronunciation – is the term given to the 'correct' pronunciation of standard English. Only a small number of people actually speak with RP. Nowadays it is often confused with 'sounding posh', whereas it was taken for granted in news reports from the 1940s and '50s.

Common misconceptions

Formal English is not the same as standard English, which is defined as the accepted form of English in any English-speaking country.

Handy tips

If you set up letter-writing exercises, try to write for a purpose; in other words, letters that may require a response. This can be external to the school, or internal. Links with drama have plenty of potential for formal letters too – the purpose can just as easily be imaginary.

Teaching ideas

● Have a weekly 'news desk', rotating children in pairs to present and tell news, general or personal, in formal English.

● Invite parents in to talk about their careers and any job interviews they may have attended. Have them talk about what it was like, how they tried to come across and how it affected their speaking.

● Work in small groups to create a radio broadcast live from the Great Fire of London.

Towards fluency and independence

Subject facts

By the time they leave primary school even the most able of children will not have fully mastered the English language. As teachers, what we want for them is a love of language in all its forms; competence and understanding in all areas (including knowledge about the language); and a growing autonomy and desire to speak, read and write well. This book has covered some of the skills and knowledge needed to achieve this. What else can we do to engender greater fluency and independence?

● Encourage children to have the confidence to talk and sing in public, through drama, concerts and performances.

● Encourage children to read widely and share their favourite books, and make sure they are enrolled at the local library.

● Persist in reading *to* the children, whether you read yourself or use audiobooks. This tends to happen less at secondary schools, but people of all ages enjoy hearing stories as much as reading them. Remind the children that libraries usually carry a good range of audiobooks, as well as print copies.

● Foster an awareness of global and national variations in English. As we know, standard English varies from country to country, and colloquial variations from UK region to region are substantial. Video is by far the most efficient way of raising awareness.

● Whether children need to write formal or colloquial English, we should encourage them to develop a personal style. This is not something achieved easily or quickly, although the best steps towards it are the different writing opportunities already mentioned, as well as exposure to a wide and varied range of language.

Handy tips

To all teachers – look after your own vocabulary too. Keep a note of new or unusual words – you never know when you might need them, and even if you don't, just enjoy the pleasure of developing your language.

Teaching ideas

● In reading, discussing and reviewing novels encourage children to try and think about the style of the author; how do they achieve what they do, and how does their choice of vocabulary help?

● Try to form links with English-speaking schools from around the world. The internet has made talking to people in other countries so much easier.

Resources

The Primary Teacher's Guide to Writing by Eileen Jones (Scholastic Ltd)
Scholastic Literacy Skills: Vocabulary (Scholastic)

Glossary

Acronym – a real or new word made by combining the initial letters of a phrase.

Adjectives – describing words, such as *black* and *large*. They describe nouns.

Adverbs – describing words, such as *quickly* and *merrily*. They describe verbs.

Affix – a morpheme that is attached to a root word to form a new word.

Analytic phonics – an approach to phonics in which the phonemes associated with particular graphemes are not pronounced in isolation.

Antonyms – words that have opposite meanings.

Aphasia – a language disorder resulting from brain trauma or disease.

Asperger's syndrome – a condition that affects social communication and interaction skills.

Aural – of or relating to the sense of hearing.

Autism – a brain disorder that affects perception of and response to the external environment.

Baseline assessment – a summative assessment aimed at establishing the ability ranges in a child or cohort, usually performed at the start of an academic year.

Blend – bringing two sounds together in a smooth flow.

Broca's area – the part of the brain used for speech production.

Cadence – the rhythm and tone of poetry.

Cerebral palsy – difficulties with motor control affecting different parts of the body.

Cliché – an overused idiom or expression.

Compound word – a new word that is created by bringing two words together as one word, hyphenated or with a space between them.

Conjunctions – used to join phrases together, such as *but* and *for*.

Core resources – provide a comprehensive solution to a curriculum subject.

Correct – the stage at which children are competent spellers, including strategies for self-correction.

Deafness – problems with hearing that may be partial or total.

Derivative – when an affix does not change the class of the word.

Determiners – used to make nouns specific.

Diagnostic assessment – a specialised assessment to identify specific difficulties.

Digraph – a combination of two graphemes that represent a single sound.

Dipthong – a phoneme consisting of two vowels that are next to each other, where the sound starts with the first vowel and moves into the next.

Dysarthria – specific problems with clear articulation of words.

Dysgraphia – a specific difficulty with writing.

Dyslexia – a learning difficulty that inhibits the ability to learn to read and write.

Dyspraxia – a neurological condition that affects coordination and movement control.

Elision – the omission of a sound or syllable.

Formal English – a tone and style of language required for formal situations.

Formative assessment – carried out with the primary objective of deciding which next steps of teaching and learning are needed.

Grapheme – the visual representation of sound, usually in letters.

Guide words – the words at the top of each page in a dictionary that allow us to see the range of words on that double-page spread.

Headword – the word under which a dictionary entry is listed.

Homographs – words that have the same spelling but are pronounced differently.

Homonyms – words that have the same spelling but have different meanings.

Homophones – words that have different spellings but the same pronunciations.

Idiom – expressions that are not meant literally.

Inflection – changing the pitch and tone of the voice, usually for expressive purposes.

Jargon – the technical language used by a particular set of people or organisation.

Language deprivation – existing in an environment with minimal linguistic stimulation.

Larynx – the voice box.

Legalese – language full of terminology pertaining to the subject.

Lexicon – the vocabulary of a particular language.

Long vowel sounds – the vowel phonemes that have a greater duration when pronounced, such as /ay/ in *able*.

Metalanguage – the technical language used to explain a subject.

Metaphor – non-literal use of language to help describe something, such as *he was stony faced*.

Metre – the structure and beats of a poem.

Mnemonic – a technique for jogging the memory.

Monosyllabic – a word with only one syllable.

Morpheme – a meaningful linguistic unit.

Mutism – being unable or unwilling to speak.

Nouns – naming words, such as *table* and *computer*. They identify objects.

Onomatopoeia – when words sound like what they stand for, such as, bark.

Onset and rime – splitting monosyllabic words into an initial consonant sound and a final vowel-based sound.

Oracy – the ability to clearly speak and understand

spoken language.

Oral – of or related to speaking.

Pedagogy – The method and practice (or art) of teaching.

Percentile score – a 'ranking' from 1–100 which usually provides a bell-curve distribution of scores when those for many children are combined.

Personification – to give human attributes to something being desribed.

Phoneme – the smallest identifiable sound in a language.

Phonetic – 1 Letter or letters that invariably represent the same sound. 2 The stage of spelling using direct grapheme/phoneme representation.

Polysyllabic – a word with more than one syllable.

Pre-communicative – the early stage of spelling, where young children show awareness of letters.

Predictive text – a devices' ability to 'guess' what word you are trying to type and to complete it or offer a range of options.

Prefix – morphemes attached to the beginning of root words.

Prepositions – indicate movement, time and place, such as *into*, *by* and *between*.

Productive (or active) vocabulary – words actively used

Pronouns – are used in place of nouns, such as *she* and *it*.

Proverb – an idiomatic saying that is complete in its own right.

Receptive (or passive) vocabulary – words that we know but don't use in everyday communication.

Root word – the primary unit of a word, sometimes referred to as the *base*.

Saxon genitive – use of the apostrophe to show possession.

Segmentation – the act of dividing or partitioning words when speaking.

Semantic – having meaning in language.

Semi-phonetic – an increasing but inconsistent awareness of the alphabet in children's writing.

Short vowel sounds – the vowel phonemes that have a shorter duration when pronounced, such as /a/ in *apple*.

Silent letters – letters which make no sound in a particular word.

Simile – a non-literal comparison using like or as, such as, *ears like radars*, or *as hard as nails*.

SMS – short message service.

Speech to text software – allows users to dictate while the software converts their voice to text. Usually the software has to be 'trained' to recognise the idiosyncrasies of each person's voice. Currently this software is expensive for schools, mainly because it requires high-performance computers to work effectively.

Spell-checker – a portable electronic device, with miniature keyboard, that allows users to check spellings. Advanced versions may include definitions and synonyms.

Spelling age – an easy-to-understand guide to show whether children are performing above, below or at their 'expected' ability.

Standardised score – as with spelling age, but with 100 as the average. These are used for statistical interpretation of large amounts of data from many children.

Stress – the syllable that receives emphasis when speaking, such as o**bey**.

Suffix – morphemes attached to the end of root words.

Summative assessment – carried out with the primary objective of establishing baselines and monitoring children's progress, and (sometimes) the performance of teachers and schools.

Supplementary resources – provide specific reinforcement, support or extension for aspects of a subject.

Syllable – a unit of pronunciation.

Syllabification – breaking down words into syllables.

Synonyms – words with identical or similar meanings.

Synthetic phonics – an approach to phonics based on learning sounds to construct words.

Textese – the language of texting (or SMS language).

Transitional – children's progression to more complex spelling skills.

Verbosity – the tendency to use too many words.

Verbs – are doing words. They identify actions, such as *throw* and *speak*.

Vocal tract – the whole structure for making sounds: the larynx and the mouth.

Vowel digraph – a combination of two vowel graphemes to represent a single sound.

Wernicke's area – the part of the brain used for understanding language.

Word family – a group of words related to each other by a combination of form, grammar and meaning.

Index

sp–vo

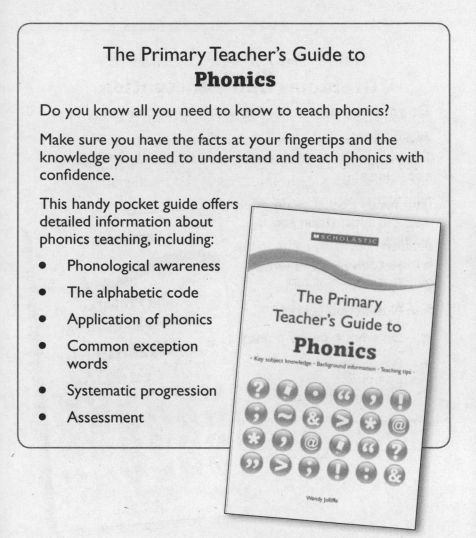

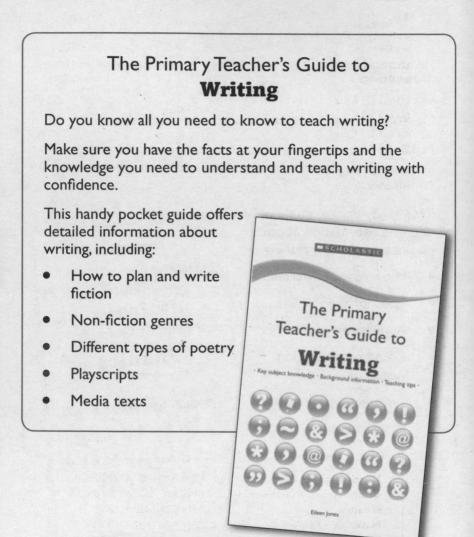

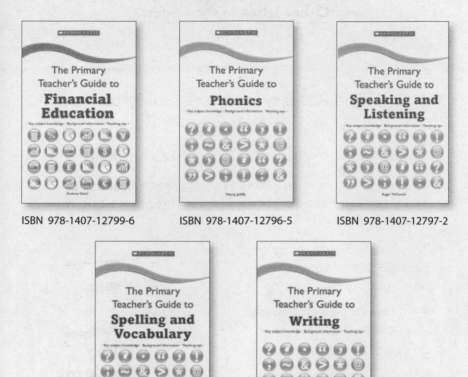